PRACTICAL
GOURMET

Company's Coming®

Smokin', Eh

Canadian Hot and Cold Smoking

Anderson • Paré • Lepine

Library and Archives Canada Cataloguing in Publication
Anderson, Ted, author
       Smokin', Eh / Ted Anderson, Jean Paré, James Darcy.

(Original series)
Includes index.
Co-published by Company's Coming.
ISBN 978-1-988133-06-5 (spiral bound)

       1. Smoking (Cooking). I. Anderson, Ted, 1980-, author
II. Darcy, James, author III. Title. IV. Series: Paré, Jean.
Original series.

TX609.P35 2016   641.6'16   C2016-901544-0

Thanks to Brad Smoliak and Jeff Morrison for their contributions to the recipes, and to Ashley Billey for her help with the nutritional information.

Distributed by
Canada Book Distributors - Booklogic
11414-119 Street
Edmonton. Alberta, Canada T5G 2X6
Tel: 1-800-661-9017

We acknowledge the financial support of the Government of Canada through the Canada Book Fund for our publishing activities.

Funded by the Government of Canada
Financé par le gouvernement du Canada | Canadä

PC: 35

Table of Contents

The Jean Paré Story

Jean Paré (pronounced "jeen PAIR-ee") grew up understanding that the combination of family, friends and home cooking is the best recipe for a good life. When Jean left home, she took with her a love of cooking, many family recipes and an intriguing desire to read cookbooks as if they were novels!

When her four children had all reached school age, Jean volunteered to cater the 50th anniversary celebration of the Vermilion School of Agriculture, now Lakeland College, in Alberta, Canada. Working out of her home, Jean prepared a dinner for more than 1,000 people, launching a flourishing catering operation that continued for over 18 years.

"Never share a recipe you wouldn't use yourself."

As requests for her recipes increased, Jean was often asked the question, "Why don't you write a cookbook?" The publication of *150 Delicious Squares* on April 14, 1981 marked the debut of what would soon become one of the world's most popular cookbook series.

Company's Coming cookbooks are distributed in Canada, the United States, Australia and other world markets. Bestsellers many times over in English, Company's Coming cookbooks have also been published in French and Spanish.

Familiar and trusted in home kitchens around the world, Company's Coming cookbooks are offered in a variety of formats. Highly regarded as kitchen workbooks, the softcover Original Series, with its lay-flat plastic comb binding, is still a favourite among readers.

Jean Paré's approach to cooking has always called for quick and easy recipes using everyday ingredients. That view has served her well.

Jean continues to share what she calls The Golden Rule of Cooking: Never share a recipe you wouldn't use yourself. It's an approach that has worked—millions of times over!

Practical Gourmet

Good company and great food create a powerful combination. When laughter and conversation mix with the heady fragrance and flavours of delicious fare, we are not just sharing a meal—we are nourishing our lives. Artfully prepared dishes awaken the senses and please the palate. And here's the secret: It can all be so simple!

Practical Gourmet is delighted to partner with **Company's Coming** to introduce a new series designed to help home cooks create no-fuss, sumptuous food. It is possible to wow both the eye and the palate using readily available ingredients and minimal effort. Practical Gourmet offers sophisticated recipes without the hassle of complicated methods, special equipment or obscure ingredients.

Titles in this series feature step-by-step instructions, full-page colour photos with every recipe, menu suggestions and sidebars on preparation tips and tricks.

Approachable recipes, fabulous results, wonderful get-togethers—it all starts with *Smokin', Eh*.

PINE RIDGE INDIANS DRYING MEAT.   COPYRIGHTED
                                 1908 BY S.D.BUTCHER & SON.

Introduction

Humans have been smoking food since the fumes rising from the caves of our ancestors brought the joy of unexpected flavours. Not only did smoke make the meat taste better, but its preservative characteristics allowed people to store their meat for times when fresh food was not as readily available. The Sumerians were smoking fish as early as 3500 BC. The remains of a smoking station from 2000 BC are located near the River Bann in Ireland. The Romans and Greeks had traditions of smoked cheese and fish that have survived to this day. The Chinese applied smoke to fruit and teas. Smoking as a method of infusing flavour and as a means of preservation is found throughout the world.

Perhaps one of the most significant reasons why Canadian traditions on smoking are different from elsewhere in the world is because of its the long history with the First Nations cultures across Canada. In particular, the seasonal spawning and migration of fish, birds and mammals provided a temporary wealth of food that required preserving for leaner times.

For the First Nations of the Canadian prairies, the extraordinary bounty of the buffalo hunt created the challenge of preserving the meat. It was often dried in the hot sun, but using a fire for heat and smoke sped up the drying process and added preservatives to the surface of the meat. Pemmican —a mixture of powdered dried meat, fat and berries packed in a rawhide sack—later became a staple for voyageurs, Métis and early settlers, who were beyond the reach of supply ships.

My grandmother smoked moose or bison on a rack covered by canvas to trap the smoke. She said the smoke was important to keep the flies away. My job as a kid was to chase away the larger wild animals attracted by the rich smell of smoked meat.

Like many of her neighbours, she later built a smokehouse that made smoking much easier. Even as refrigeration displaced the old ways, her jerky and pemmican were celebrated at feasts, powwows and gatherings.

Grandmother's Cree and Métis ancestors had perfected smoking bison and then pounding the dried meat into a powder so they could make pemmican. On a cold winter afternoon as we came in from the cold, she would serve us a smoky, fatty rubaboo stew—a mouthwatering, hearty dish to warm us.

Many other First Nations peoples across Canada have a rich history of smoking food. The Beothuk people of Newfoundland used an arrangement of fences to drive caribou to the hunters. When the hunt yielded an abundance of meat, they built smokehouses about 10 feet long in which they would dry and preserve the game. They then packed it in birch containers for storage.

The coastal peoples of Canada had the bounty of the spawning runs of salmon, char, steelhead and herring. They learned to perfect the more delicate process of cooler smoking to preserve the fish without overly breaking down the interior flesh. The smoke prevented the surface oils from turning rancid and created a perfect combination of flavours. I love to enter a well-used west coast smokehouse filled with its heavy fragrance of air I feel I could eat.

Smoking traditions continued to develop as immigrants arrived in Canada, bringing their own smoking methods while adapting their techniques and recipes to the Aboriginal customs and to the unique wild game and wood species of Canada.

Each year our family smokes mussels on pine needles over a cedar plank in much the way Champlain would have done when he established L'Ordre de Bon Temps in 1606 in the new settlement at Port-Royal.

Quebecois have a long tradition in certain areas of smoking ham by hanging it in the chimney, giving further rise to one of my favourite dishes, Habitant soup. The Romanian and Eastern European immigrants to Montreal brought their traditions of brining and smoking that gave us the unique brisket now called Montreal smoked meat. Great traditions of cheese making survived in monasteries and led us to new discoveries of blue and ripened smoked cheeses.

In much the same way as the unique character of Canadian smoking was crafted around the nation's wild fish, mammals and birds, the availability of wild berries and plants was responsible for unique sauces, rubs and condiments. Berries of juniper, Saskatoon, currant, chokecherry and blueberry have remained in Canadian cuisine along with smoked pine needles and leaves of wild tea. Smoked tomatoes and peppers also commonly find their way into our slathering sauces.

The next great difference in Canadian smoking tradition stems from the wood of the northern trees we have exploited in the quest for the perfect combination of heat and flavour. Maple-smoked bacon is a classic, along with apple wood-smoked cheddar and alder-smoked salmon and salt. The wood of cherry trees adds sweet perfume to our dishes, and oak and birch are staples of our northern smoking heritage.

While we do use imported southern woods from the United States, such as pecan, hickory and mesquite, our local woods provide inexpensive fuel to enhance our local cuisine.

During the winter, Canadians might be tempted to use their barbeques in a different way rather than having to tend a high-heat grill that requires constant attention. I've been to great feasts in full-blown Canadian winters where the host dashes to the warmth of the smoker only occasionally to check the water bath or the coals. Mid-winter smoking can be a delight of cooking without looking.

Regional American Styles of Barbecue (Smoking)

In the United States, traditional barbecuing refers to indirect cooking using smoke and heat as opposed to grilling, which uses higher direct heat.

The southeastern and south central parts of the U.S. are the core regions of the American barbecue tradition. Although barbecue restaurants are found outside this area, most of the top ones have their origins there. Each of the southern barbecue regions has distinct techniques and ingredients.

Kansas City barbecue uses a wide variety of meats stemming from the city's history as a meat-packing centre. It is smoked low and slow over hickory, and the higher-fat burnt ends of the brisket are especially prized. The sauce is a thick, sweet and tangy combination of tomato, molasses and spices that stick to the ribs and the pallet.

The typical North Carolina pork barbecue is often brushed with a combination of vinegar and spices, but each locale has its own variation. The western part of the state serves the meat in heavier ketchup, the eastern part in vinegar-based sauces. The Lexington barbecue in the centre of the state uses a combination of vinegar and ketchup with a specialty of pork ribs and shoulder.

South Carolina is a rarity in that it uses four types of traditional barbecue sauces: light and heavy tomato-based, vinegar based and mustard-based sauces.

The barbecue of Kentucky is dry-rubbed and smoked with hickory, and the sauce is served on the side.

The barbecues of Tennessee, Georgia and Alabama typically use a sweet tomato-based sauce, although micro-regional variations are found in northern Alabama, where they often use a mayonnaise and vinegar–based white sauce on chicken and pork. Memphis smokehouses use a dry rub that includes paprika, garlic and other spices, although the tomato- and vinegar-based sauces also feature in their barbecue tradition. The meat is often cooked in a large pit, and the pulled pork sandwich is a specialty.

Central Texas or Austin-style barbecue was influenced by German and Czech immigrants from the mid-1800s and is dry-rubbed and smoked over pecan and oak in a simple un-sauced style. Traditional smokehouses do not typically provide cutlery with their barbecue; the briskets, ribs and sausages are eaten with the fingers and served with bread to sop up the juices. East Texas beef is marinated in a sweet tomato-based sauce and slow cooked over hickory until it is super tender. South Texas uses heavy molasses sauces to create a moist meat, and West Texas "cowboy-style" barbecue is most often cooked over mesquite wood with direct heat so it is grilled rather than barbecued (smoked).

Hot Smoking

Technically, if you smoke your food above 140°F (60°C), you are hot smoking. This form of smoking is the most common and has the most application in terms of the variety of foods that can be cooked. Brisket is the quintessential cut of meat for smoking, but most pork, beef, poultry and even game meat is delicious cooked in a smoker.

When food is hot smoked, it is cooked with ambient heat while being infused with smoke. The smoke does not actually cook the meat; it just provides the flavour. For best results, your heat source should be smouldering (no open flames!), and it should not be directly under the food being cooked.

Hot smoked food is fully cooked and ready to eat once it comes out of the smoker. Meat cooked at temperatures ranging from 140°F to 176°F (60 to 80°C) remains moist because the temperature is not high enough to render out the fat. Meat cooked above 200°F (93°C) requires a source of moisture in the smoker to keep it from drying out. A pan of water, apple juice or beer placed near your heat source will add steam to the smoke, ensuring a moist final product. You can get a similar result by spritzing your meat periodically as it cooks, but be sure to close the lid as quickly as possible to maintain the temperature in the smoker and so as not to lose too much smoke.

Obviously, with smoking, the quality of the smoke determines the quality and flavour of the food. You can tell a lot about how your food will taste by the colour of the smoke coming from your smoker. Ideally a pale bluish smoke, which has the smallest particle size, will impart a nice, lightly smoked flavour. White smoke also has relatively small particles and will still provide tasty results. Grey smoke, however, is made up of large particles of unburned fuel and will give your food an overpowering smoky flavour.

Cold Smoking

Cold smoking does not enjoy the same popularity as hot smoking, in part because it is a bit trickier to master, but also because it does not have as wide an application. However, when done properly, cold smoking produces mouth-wateringly moist cheeses, fish and seafood, and can also be used with nuts and fruit.

Cold smokers generally have two chambers, one for the fire and one for the food. A pipe connects the fire chamber to the food chamber so the smoke fills the food chamber without adding heat. Cold smoking can be done in a regular smoker, too, but it can be a challenge to keep the temperature in the smoker low enough.

The most important thing to remember about cold smoking is that this process does not cook the food. Temperatures in a cold smoker are too low to kill pathogens. The smoke does not cook food; it just adds flavour. In cold smoking, temperatures generally range from 65 to 85°F (18 to 60°C), far below the threshold for pasteurization (130°F/ 55°C).

CAUTION: If done improperly, cold smoking can put food into the so-called "danger zone" for bacteria growth, which is from 40 to 140°F (4 to 60°C). Food within this temperature range is warm enough to allow bacteria to grow quickly but not hot enough to kill them. To be safe for consumption, any food to be cold smoked should be cured before it is smoked or cooked after it comes out of the smoker.

Smoking Techniques

Brining

Brining is a great method to add salt and other seasonings to your food. A simple brine consists only of water and a low percentage of salt; through osmosis, some of the salt and water are absorbed into the food, keeping it very moist during and after cooking. Brining will change the texture of fresh meat and fish though, yielding a firm, cured-like product when cooked.

Dry rubs

Dry rubs are the other form of applying seasoning to food when smoking. Very common in the world of barbecue, a dry rub contains salt, sugar, herbs and spices. The food is seasoned (normally quite generously) with the rub before cooking, sometimes even a few days ahead of time, to allow more penetration of the rub into the food and to pull moisture out of the food, giving it a "cured" flavour and texture.

Mops

Mops are used to add moisture or glaze food in your smoker. I don't make mention of them specifically in this book, but we do advocate brushing sauce on food a few times during the cooking.

Pellicle

A pellicle is a thin layer of dried protein on a piece of meat or fish. This layer helps smoke "stick" to the food during the smoking process. The normal way of creating the pellicle is to refrigerate the food on a rack, uncovered, overnight or until that layer is created. When touched, the pellicle should have a slightly dry and tacky feel to it.

Pull test

The "pull test" is a well-known indicator of doneness in slow and low cooking circles. To perform a pull test on a rack of ribs, grasp a rib in the thickest area of the slab and gently twist and pull that bone from side to side. When the meat is cooked just right, the bone will just begin to loosen from the meat, a true sign of "pull off the bone" doneness. If the bone moves really easily, that indicates "fall off the bone" doneness, which is generally viewed as overcooked.

Spritzing

Again, not mentioned a whole lot in the book, but it is helpful to have a spray bottle of water (or other liquid—apple juice, beer, whiskey) nearby mist the food you are smoking every once and a while. It's worth remembering that when smoking food, we are building flavour a little bit at a time.

Wrapping

Also known as the "Texas crutch," wrapping large cuts of meat in foil part way through cooking speeds up cooking and mimics braising in a sealed Dutch oven. Advocates of this technique insist that wrapping is the superior way to cook briskets, pork butts, ribs or any other big pieces of meat. Give it a try once or twice, and make your own judgment.

A Final Word...

They say that experience is the best teacher—very true when it comes to smoking. food. These recipes are great guidelines, giving quantities of salt, spices, temperatures, fuel sources and timing, but experience will dictate what you may do the next time you smoke that fish. Your smoking device will behave differently than mine or your neighbour's. I encourage you to smoke often and note what techniques have worked for you, and what needs improvement. I've been smoking food for years but every time I put something into my smoker, I am aiming to make it taste better than the last time, based on my experience.

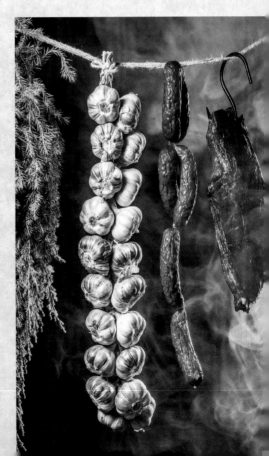

Sticky Soy Sauce Beef Ribs

A powerhouse dish with stunning presentation. The bones are meaty and savoury, and will impress your guests, piled up on a platter, glossy and with an incredible aroma. Simple Crunchy Coleslaw (p.138) is a perfect side dish for these ribs, just a little something to cut through the richness of the beef. Fried shallots can be found in most Asian grocery stores.

Racks of beef back ribs (about 4 lbs., 1.8 kg, each)	2	2
Sea salt	2 tsp.	10 mL
Light soy sauce	1 cup	250 mL
Fish sauce	1/4 cup	60 mL
Brown sugar, packed	1/2 cup	125 mL
Garlic cloves, smashed	5	5
Cranks of black pepper	10	10
Cornstarch	2 tbsp.	30 mL
Water	2 tbsp.	30 mL
Green onions, finely sliced on a bias	4	4
Toasted, unhulled sesame seeds	1 tbsp.	15 mL
Fried shallots	1 cup	250 mL

Remove the membrane from the back of the ribs. Season the ribs with sea salt on both sides and chill in the fridge overnight.

For the sauce, combine the next 5 ingredients in a medium saucepot and bring to a simmer. Let simmer gently for about 5 minutes.

Make a slurry with the cornstarch and water, then add 3/4 to the sauce. Simmer until the sauce is thick and glossy; if it looks too runny, add the rest of the slurry and simmer again. Remove the garlic cloves and chill the sauce until you need it.

Preheat your smoking device to 220°F (105°C) using oak. Smoke the ribs for 8 hours, basting every hour after the first 5 hours. Do a pull test (see p. 15) to see if they are tender.

Place the meat on a cutting board, bone side down, and cut into individual ribs. Right before serving, sprinkle with green onion, sesame seeds and fried shallots. Makes 6 servings.

1 serving: 870 Calories; 30 g Total Fat (12 g Mono, 2 g Poly, 10 g Sat); 270 mg Cholesterol; 41 g Carbohydrate (1 g Fibre, 22 g Sugar); 106 g Protein; 3370 mg Sodium

Slow-smoked Prime Rib of Beef

Prime rib is such a crowd pleaser, and this version is no exception. Use the highest grade of beef you can find; dry-aged meat is a bonus. When the meat is slowly brought to a perfect medium-rare interior, you and your guests will marvel at the way the smoke seems to intensify the richness of this exquisite cut. We finish it with a herbaceous garlic butter to bring a touch of freshness, and to compliment the beefiness of this, the king of roasts.

Prime rib, bone in (about 3 lbs., 1.4 kg)	1	1
Sea salt, to taste		
Freshly ground black pepper, to taste		
Garlic and Parsley Butter (see p. 154), softened	4 1/2 oz.	125 g

Preheat your smoking device to 200°F (95°C) using cherry wood and charcoal.

Season beef heavily with salt and pepper, rubbing the seasoning into the meat with your hands. Insert a thermometer probe into the thickest part of the meat and place on a smoking rack, if using. Smoke the beef until it reaches the desired internal temperature (about 2 hours for medium-rare): 120°F (50°C) for rare, 130°F (55°C) for medium-rare, 140°F (60°C) for medium and 150°F (65°C) for medium-well.

Remove the beef from your smoker and slather it with parsley butter, then wrap it in aluminum foil and set aside to rest for 20 minutes.

For a crusty outside, omit the butter step and let the meat rest for 20 minutes. Quickly sear it in a cast iron pan, or on a hot barbecue, then slather with parsley butter. Keep in mind the beef is cooked perfectly, so do not keep it on the heat for long! Finally, carve the roast off the bone, slice into servings and sprinkle with a little salt. Makes 6 servings.

1 serving: 740 Calories; 60 g Total Fat (23 g Mono, 2.5 g Poly, 28 g Sat); 205 mg Cholesterol; trace Carbohydrate (0 g Fibre, 0 g Sugar); 46 g Protein; 850 mg Sodium

A flaked sea salt such as Maldon (from England), fleur de sel (France), or better yet, Canadian fleur de sel (Vancouver Island), will add a great textural component to the sliced meat, while seasoning it at the same time.

Smoked Pepper Steak

This recipe is a great addition to a poker or games night with friends. Not too complicated or pretentious, it's a thick, heavily peppered steak with a tender and tasty result. Feel free to mix up the peppercorns used—briny green peppercorns are a great twist to this meaty main.

Lemon juice	2 tsp.	10 mL
Cooking oil	2 tsp.	10 mL
Worcestershire sauce	1 tsp.	5 mL
Garlic clove, minced	1	1
Seasoned salt	1/4 tsp.	1 mL
Top sirloin steak, about 1 1/2 inches, 3.8 cm, thick (about 2 1/4 lbs., 1 kg) see Note	1	1
Crushed black peppercorns	2 tbsp.	30 mL

Preheat your smoking device to 300°F (150°C) using mesquite wood. Combine the first 5 ingredients in a small bowl and brush over both sides of the steak. Firmly press the peppercorns into both sides of the meat using the heel of your hand. Place the steak on a greased smoking rack. Smoke the beef, turning once, until it reaches the desired internal temperature (about 40 minutes for medium-rare): 120°F (50°C) for rare, 130°F (55°C) for medium-rare, 140°F (60°C) for medium and 150°F (65°C) for medium-well. Let the beef stand for 15 minutes before cutting across the grain into 1/8 inch (3 mm) slices. Makes 8 servings.

1 serving: 290 Calories; 21 g Total Fat (10 g Mono, 1 g Poly, 8 g Sat); 90 mg Cholesterol; 1 g Carbohydrate (0 g Fibre, 0 g Sugar); 26 g Protein; 150 mg Sodium

Note: You will need to special order this thickness of steak from your butcher.

Smoked Strip Loin

I love smoked beef—it has a fantastic flavour, and it's good hot or cold, sliced thin or thick. You can prepare this recipe for a large party, and it's a great alternative to the normal turkey or ham for holiday dinners.

Brown sugar	1/4 cup	60 mL
Sugar	1/4 cup	60 mL
Seasoning salt	1/4 cup	60 mL
Paprika	1/4 cup	60 mL
Garlic salt	2 tbsp.	30 mL
Chili powder	1 tbsp.	15 mL
Freshly ground pepper	1 tbsp.	15 mL
Onion salt	1 tbsp.	15 mL
Celery salt	1 1/2 tsp.	7 mL
Allspice	1/2 tsp.	2 mL
Cayenne pepper	1/2 tsp.	2 mL
Strip loin roast (about 4 1/2 lbs., 2 kg)	1	1

For the rub, combine the first 11 ingredients in a medium bowl.

Pat the meat dry, then coat with rub, making sure you get some rub in all creases and folds (you won't need all the rub). Put the roast in a baking dish and refrigerate for at least 6 hours.

Preheat your smoking device to 300°F (150x°C) with cherry wood. Smoke the beef until it reaches the desired internal temperature (about 90 minutes for medium-rare): 120°F (50°C) for rare, 130°F (55°C) for medium-rare, 140°F (60°C) for medium and 150°F (65°C) for medium-well. Allow the roast to rest for 15 minutes before carving. Makes 7 servings.

1 serving: 470 Calories; 15 g Total Fat
(6 g Mono, 1 g Poly, 5 g Sat); 140 mg Cholesterol;
7 g Carbohydrate (0 g Fibre, 2 g Sugar);
62 g Protein; 1700 mg Sodium

Smoked Brisket

The brisket is infamous for being the most difficult of cuts to master the cooking of. Truly, experience is a great teacher with this piece of meat, but I have a few hints that will make your first time cooking it be rewarding and leave you wanting to do it again! This particular preparation owes it's flavour profile to Montreal smoked meat, with mustard seed and black pepper in the rub. It will take 10 to 12 hours to cook the brisket properly, so make sure to plan accordingly.

Black peppercorns	2 tbsp.	30 mL
Coriander seed	1 tbsp.	15 mL
Fennel seed	1 tbsp.	15 mL
Mustard seed	3 tbsp.	45 mL
Caraway seed	1 tbsp.	15 mL
Medium onion, peeled and cut into chunks	1	1
Head of garlic, peeled	1	1
Salt	1/3 cup	75 mL
Brown sugar	1/3 cup	75 mL
Paprika	4 tsp.	20 mL
Beef brisket (about 11 lbs., 5 kg) (see Tip)	1	1

Pulse the first 5 ingredients in a coffee grinder until finely ground.

Combine the next 4 ingredients in the bowl of a food processor and pulse until finely chopped. Add the ground spices and paprika and pulse until combined.

Lay out 3 overlapping lengths of plastic wrap on your counter, ensuring that they are longer than the brisket. Slather the brisket with the onion and spice paste, using all of the paste. Lay some plastic wrap on top of the brisket, then fold up the bottom sides of the wrap, creating a sealed package of meat and seasoning. Place in a container large enough to hold any leaks, should they occur, and refrigerate overnight.

Preheat your smoking device to 250°F (120°C) using oak wood. Allow the brisket to warm at room temperature while the smoker is preheating, for about 1 hour. Unwrap the brisket, insert a probe thermometer into the thickest part of the meat and place into the smoker. Cooking time will vary based on weight and shape of the meat, consistent temperature of the cooker and temperature outside. You want an internal temperature of 185°F (85°C) as an indicator to start testing. At this point, use a toothpick to judge tenderness—it should slide in and out of the meat very easily. Once the brisket is cooked, wrap it tightly in aluminum foil and let it rest on a cutting board for 30 to 60 minutes. Slice across the grain (across the width of the brisket) into 1/4 inch (6 mm) slices. Makes 12 servings.

Tip: Buy the highest quality, highest grade brisket you can find, from a reputable butcher that you trust. Quality WILL make a difference here; you can disguise a poor quality steak with marinade/sauces, etc., but a brisket will speak for itself. Ask your butcher to trim it for you, leaving 1/3 inch (1 cm) of fat across the top but removing any large fat deposits. The fat is important for moist, succulent meat, but too much may not render out properly, resulting in a poor eating experience.

1 serving: 700 Calories; 32 g Total Fat (15 g Mono, 1 g Poly, 11 g Sat); 205 mg Cholesterol; 11 g Carbohydrate (2 g Fibre, 7 g Sugar); 88 g Protein; 3840 mg Sodium

Only good things come out of leftover brisket—sandwiches, omelettes and, my personal favourite, hash. Sauté a diced onion and a few leftover potatoes, add some chopped garlic and diced leftover brisket, and finish with chopped herbs and a couple of soft poached eggs.

Smoked Bacon-wrapped Meatloaf

Meatloaf was hardly my most anticipated meal when I was growing up (sorry Mum); I was always thinking about hamburgers when eating it. That feeling stayed with me for many years, until a sous-chef of mine made me her version. I never realized that meatloaf could be so tender and full of flavour—the caramelized ketchup on the outside of the bacon is key. This is a close approximation to how Jane used to make it, tweaked for a slow cook in a smoker.

Olive oil	1 tbsp.	15 mL
Medium onion, minced	1/2	1/2
Garlic cloves, minced	3	3
Bread crumbs	2 1/3 cups	575 mL
Fresh rosemary leaves, finely chopped	1 tsp.	5 mL
Water	2/3 cup	150 mL
Egg, beaten	1	1
Gouda, grated	1/4 cup	60 mL
Ketchup	6 tbsp.	90 mL
Black pepper, freshly ground	1/4 tsp	1 mL
Salt	1/2 tbsp.	7 mL
Ground beef, regular	1 3/4 lbs.	800 g
Bacon slices	12	12

Heat the olive oil in a medium saucepot on medium. Add the minced onion and garlic and cook for about 3 to 4 minutes, until softened and just starting to brown. Add the bread crumbs and rosemary and cook, stirring, for another 3 to 4 minutes, until the bread crumbs absorb the oil and begin to brown as well. Remove from heat and allow to cool to room temperature.

In a large mixing bowl, stir the next 5 ingredients and bread crumb mixture until you have a paste. Mix in the ground beef until all ingredients have just fully incorporated. Chill for 1 hour, to firm it up.

Preheat your smoking device to 300°F (150°C) using maple wood. Lay 2 sheets of parchment paper, each about 10 inches (25 cm) long, on your work surface. Spread 3 tbsp. (45 mL) of ketchup on each sheet in a rectangle about 7 inches (18 cm) wide and 4 inches (10 cm) tall. Next, using the ketchup as a guide, lay 6 strips of bacon down vertically on the parchment paper, slightly overlapping, and top with half the meatloaf mixture, keeping it centred. Bring the bottom edge up towards the top edge and roll the meatloaf in the bacon, tucking the leading edge of the bacon underneath the meatloaf as you roll to create a neat, tidy tube shape.

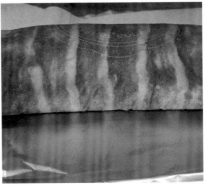

Lay bacon over ketchup and top with meatloaf mixture.

Roll into a tidy tube shape.

Roll in foil and twist ends tightly.

Let rest for 15 minutes before slicing.

Continue rolling so the parchment paper is in the same shape, then twist the ends of the paper tightly. Repeat for the other roll.

Lay out 2 sheets of aluminum foil large enough to encompass both rolls. Lay 1 parchment roll on each foil sheet, then roll it on itself until you have a neat and tidy tube shape and twist the ends tightly.

Smoke for 1 hour, or until a thermometer inserted into the centre of the meatloaf reads 140°F (60°C). Gently remove the foil and paper, taking care as the meatloaf will be delicate to handle. Continue smoking until the internal temperature reaches 165°F (75°C) and the meatloaf has a lovely golden brown colour on the outside. Let it rest for 15 minutes before slicing, being sure to keep it covered to retain its heat. Makes 6 servings.

1 serving: 990 Calories; 73 g Total Fat (33 g Mono, 4.5 g Poly, 27 g Sat); 180 mg Cholesterol; 45 g Carbohydrate (2 g Fibre, 9 g Sugar); 40 g Protein; 2210 mg Sodium

🥢 While delicious with the traditional accompaniments of mashed potatoes, gravy and steamed greens, I would highly recommend the "hot meatloaf sandwich" option. Take a thick slice of country bread, toast it heavily, brush it with butter, place a slice or two of meatloaf on top and smother it with gravy. Accompany that with a crisp green salad, and dinner is served!

Smoky Beef Jerky

Homemade jerky is fantastic. I like being able to control what ingredients go in the marinade—no preservatives, other than salt and wood smoke. This tasty, dense form of protein is a great companion on a hike or a long bike ride. It is also a tasty appetizer for your guests to munch on with a cold beer while the main course is on the grill. A fragrant hickory aroma and savoury spice makes this jerky hard to resist.

Soy sauce	1/3 cup	75 mL
Bourbon whisky	1/4 cup	60 mL
Brown sugar, packed	1/4 cup	60 mL
White vinegar	1/4 cup	60 mL
Worcestershire sauce	2 tbsp.	30 mL
Chili powder	1 tbsp.	15 mL
Garlic powder	1 tbsp.	15 mL
Louisiana hot sauce	2 tsp.	10 mL
Pepper	2 tsp.	10 mL
Flank steak, trimmed of fat, thinly sliced across the grain (1/8 inch, 3 mm, slices)	1 lb.	454 g

For the marinade, combine the first 9 ingredients in a medium bowl.

Put the beef into a large resealable freezer bag and pour the marinade over top. Seal the bag and turn until the meat is well coated. Marinate in the fridge for at least 6 hours or overnight, turning occasionally.

Remove the beef from the bag and discard any remaining marinade. Preheat your smoking device to 200°F (95°C) using hickory wood. Arrange the beef evenly on a rack that will fit in your smoker, and smoke for about 2 hours, until the beef is dried but still flexible. Cool completely. Makes about 35 pieces.

1 piece: 35 Calories; 1 g Total Fat (0 g Mono, 0 g Poly, 0 g Sat); 5 mg Cholesterol; 2 g Carbohydrate (0 g Fibre, 2 g Sugar); 3 g Protein; 170 mg Sodium

Offset Barrel Smokers

Types of Smokers

Cabinet Smokers

Bradley Smoker

The Bradley smoker is a Canadian original, developed in BC in the 1970s. Essentially, it automatically feeds wood pucks on to a burner to generate smoke for cooking in its cabinet. There are electronic models that control the temperature with an electric burner and thermostat. A very user friendly unit that creates good smoked food.

Electric and Propane Cabinet Smokers

There are many cabinet type smokers on the market, some heated with propane, some with an electric burner. They tend to have a pan in which to burn smoker chips, and a well sealed cabinet in which to smoke. Temperature is controlled with the amount of gas/electricity used to heat the cabinet. User friendly.

Little Chief and Big Chief Smokers

The Little Chief and Big Chief smokers have been popular since their inception in 1968. In this design, a pan of wood chips sits on a simple electric burner and smoulders. There isn't really an effective method of temperature control; in fact in the colder months, most users surround the smoker with the cardboard box it originally came in to act as an insulator to ensure the food is smoked hot enough. These models are very popular with anglers and hunters, as they can easily smoke a good amount of fish, jerky or sausage with very little effort.

Gas Grill and Smoker Box

You can create a smoker environment with a gas grill using a bit of technique and a smoker box—a metal box with several perforations and a hinged lid. To use the box, turn one side of the grill to low or medium-low heat and place the smoker box over the lit burner. Have a water pan underneath whatever is being smoked, and you'll have a humid and smoky environment in which to cook.

Kettle Grill

Popularized by Weber, the kettle style grill is the most versatile, and possibly the most challenging, piece of equipment to smoke with. It requires constant maintenance, yet the challenge can be well rewarded with magnificently smoked food. And, its best feature is that you can grill with it as well.

Offset Barrel Smokers

This unit is fantastic. It is also a combination grill and smoker, but is easier to manage when in smoking mode. Burn charcoal, wood chunks or even small logs in the offset firebox, adjust the dampers, and you're set.

Kettle Grill

Pellet Smokers

Pellet fed cookers tend to be expensive but offer superb control of temperature, and the fuel burns very clean, so the food has light to medium smoke flavour. They work by feeding pellets from an auger into a burn area. The heat is thermostatically controlled—some more advanced units can even use a thermometer in the food to determine when to stop heating the unit.

Smokey Mountain Cooker

To me, these vertical barrel type cookers are the most efficient out there. The amount of food that can be smoked per square inch of unit footprint is amazing. They use a water pan in the bottom, combined with charcoal and wood chips to keep the cooking environment moist and smoky for hours. Use the two dampers to control the temperature.

Szechuan Pepper Smoked Pork Belly

This preparation was inspired by a now-closed restaurant in Vancouver that used to serve this amazing pork belly, simply sliced with some rice crackers, fresh herbs and hot sauce. Be creative with it—stuff it inside steamed buns, fry it up like bacon on a sandwich, or just serve it sliced, licking the juices from your fingertips! Pairs wonderfully with Quick Pickled Cucumbers (p. 140). Feel free to use other peppercorns in place of Szechuan, if you like.

Sea salt	2 1/2 tbsp.	37 mL
Szechuan peppercorns, crushed	4 tsp.	20 mL
Granulated sugar	2 1/2 tbsp.	37 mL
Garlic cloves, peeled and chopped	4	4
Slab of pork belly, skinned (2 1/4 lbs., 1 kg)	1	1

For the cure, mix the first 4 ingredients in a mixing bowl.

Place the pork belly and cure in a non-reactive baking tray or resealable freezer bag, and massage the meat with the mixture. Cover the tray or seal the bag and place in the fridge for 12 hours.

Preheat your smoking device to 225°F (110°C) using alder wood. Rinse and pat dry the meat and place it on a rack for smoking. Smoke for about 6 hours, or until a knife can pierce the meat with no resistance. Makes 7 servings.

1 serving: 740 Calories; 76 g Total Fat (35 g Mono, 8 g Poly, 28 g Sat); 105 mg Cholesterol; 1 g Carbohydrate (0 g Fibre, trace Sugar); 13 g Protein; 500 mg Sodium

Smoked Pork Butt

The classic American barbecue dish. A large, flavourful cut of pork is seasoned well, slowly smoked, then pulled. Although traditionally piled high on a soft bun with a delicious sauce (Apricot and Mustard Barbecue Sauce [p. 146] would be a great choice), pulled pork isn't defined by sandwiches; it's great in omelettes or savoury pies, or even on pancakes for breakfast.

Coriander seed	1 tsp.	5 mL
Cumin seed	1 tsp.	5 mL
Mustard seeds	1 tsp.	5 mL
Sea salt	2 tbsp.	30 mL
Brown sugar	1/3 cup	75 mL
Freshly ground black pepper	1/4 tsp.	1 mL
Onion powder	1 tsp.	5 mL
Garlic powder	1/2 tsp.	2 mL
Mild paprika	1 tbsp.	15 mL
Cayenne pepper	1/4 tsp.	1 mL
Whole pork butt (about 8 lbs., 3.6 kg)	1	1
Yellow mustard	1 tbsp.	15 mL

For the rub, grind the coriander, cumin and mustard seeds into a powder. Combine with the next 7 ingredients and mix well.

Slather the meat with the mustard. Season the pork butt aggressively with the rub, rubbing it into the mustard so it will create a dark, crusty "bark" on the outside once cooked.

Preheat your smoking device to 225°F (110°C) using apple wood. Place the meat on a smoking rack, if using, and insert a thermometer probe into the thickest part. Place the meat into the smoker. Smoke until the internal temperature reaches 200°F (95°C), about 6 to 8 hours.

Let the meat rest for 30 minutes wrapped in aluminum foil, then shred with gloved hands, or 2 forks, and serve. Makes 10 servings.

1 serving: 570 Calories; 24 g Total Fat (11 g Mono, 2.5 g Poly, 8 g Sat); 230 mg Cholesterol; 7 g Carbohydrate (trace Fibre, 6 g Sugar); 77 g Protein; 1590 mg Sodium

Pork and Swiss Chard Cannelloni

The "worst" thing about smoking a pork butt is that there are almost always leftovers! This Italian-inspired dish is straightforward to put together and freezes very well.

Ingredient	Imperial	Metric
Olive oil	2 tbsp.	30 mL
Medium onion, minced	1	1
Swiss chard leaves, stems separated from leaves, cut in 1/2 inch (6 mm) slices	10	10
Garlic cloves, minced	4	4
Ricotta cheese	1 1/8 cup	280 mL
Grana padano cheese, grated	1/4 cup	60 mL
Smoked Pork Butt (see p. 34)	1 2/3 cups	400 mL
Large egg, lightly beaten	1	1
Lemon, zested	1	1
Salt	1 1/2 tsp	7 mL
Black pepper, freshly ground	1 tsp.	5 mL
9 oz. (250 g) package of cannelloni shells	1	1
Strained tomatoes	4 cups	1 L
Fresh mozzarella cheese, sliced 1/4 inch (6 mm) thick	7 oz.	200 g

In a heavy-bottomed pot, heat the olive oil on medium. Add the onion and chard stems and cook, stirring, for about 5 minutes, until softened. Add the garlic and cook for another 4 to 5 minutes. Turn the heat to medium-high and add the chard leaves. Cook, stirring, for another few minutes, until the chard has wilted and the liquid has evaporated. Remove from heat and cool to room temperature, then chill in the fridge for 1 hour.

In a large mixing bowl combine the next 5 ingredients and cooled chard mixture until well incorporated. Season with salt and pepper.

Flood the bottom of a large baking dish with half of the strained tomatoes. Fill each cannelloni tube with the pork mixture and lay them tightly together, filling the whole baking dish. Pour the remaining sauce over the pasta and sprinkle the mozzarella cheese evenly over top. Bake in a 350°F (175°C) oven for about 45 minutes, until the top of the dish has browned and a sharp knife easily passes through the pasta and is hot to the touch after being inserted. Let the pasta rest in the dish for 5 to 10 minutes before serving. Makes 6 sevings.

1 serving: 460 Calories; 17 g Total Fat (6 g Mono, 1.5 g Poly, 7 g Sat); 90 mg Cholesterol; 47 g Carbohydrate (5 g Fibre, 15 g Sugar); 28 g Protein; 1230 mg Sodium

Try using the cold leftover cannelloni like pate—spread it on some toasted country bread that's been rubbed with raw garlic, and drizzled with olive oil.

Pistachio-crusted Pork Side Ribs

Pork side (or spare) ribs could possibly be my favourite cut of meat to smoke. There is a great balance of fat, meat and collagen that leads to a very enjoyable eating experience. The sauce, loaded with fresh cherries and rye, is deftly balanced by the crunchy, salty pistachios. Ask your butcher for "St. Louis" cut ribs.

Slabs of pork side ribs (about 5 lbs., 2.3 kg, total)	2	2
Sea salt	3 tbsp.	45 mL
Brown sugar	1/4 cup	60 mL
Onion powder	1 tsp.	5 mL
Garlic powder	1/2 tsp.	2 mL
Paprika	4 tsp.	20 mL
Chili flakes	1/2 tsp.	2 mL
Freshly ground black pepper	1 tsp.	5 mL
Fresh savoury (use 1/2 tsp., 2 mL, dry if necessary)	1 tsp.	5 mL
Whole grain mustard	2 tbsp.	30 mL
Cherry and Rye Whisky Barbecue Sauce (see p. 144)	2 cups	500 mL
Pistachios, roasted, shelled and chopped	1/2 cup	125 mL

Place the ribs flesh side up on a cutting board and trim off any loose bits of meat so they appear neat and tidy.

For the rub, mix the next 8 ingredients in a medium mixing bowl until well combined.

Slather the mustard over both sides of the ribs, then coat liberally with the rub (you won't need all the rub). Place the ribs on a smoker rack and preheat your smoking device to 225°F (110°C) using cherry wood.

Cook for about 6 hours, and start basting with barbecue sauce every 30 minutes after 4 hours cooking. Check for tenderness at 5 hours.

When finished, glaze one last time, sprinkle with chopped pistachios, then cut ribs between the bones. Makes 2 servings.

1 serving: 1610 Calories; 122 g Total Fat (54 g Mono, 15 g Poly, 42 g Sat); 355 mg Cholesterol; 43 g Carbohydrate (8 g Fibre, 26 g Sugar); 86 g Protein; 10150 mg Sodium

Tip: Leftover rub is a great pantry item to have. Try it sprinkled on roasted vegetables, pizza or, my favourite, popcorn!

Slather the meat with musturd and coat with the rub.

Glaze one last time and sprinkle with chopped pistachios.

Cut ribs between the bones and serve.

Smoked Ribs

I find that most meats come to life when prepared in a smoker, and none are more popular than baby back ribs. Even side ribs do very well in the smoker, but there is just something special about the taste and texture of smoked baby back ribs.

Honey mustard	1/4 cup	60 mL
Chili powder	2 tbsp.	30 mL
Paprika	3 tbsp.	45 mL
Brown sugar	4 tbsp.	60 mL
Salt	1 tbsp.	15 mL
Racks of baby back ribs (about 3 lbs. 1.4 kg, total)	2	2

Combine the first 5 ingredients in a medium bowl and mix well. Rub mixture all over ribs and place in a cooler or fridge for about 1 hour.

Preheat smoker to 200°F (95°C) using maple wood and place the ribs in the cooking chamber. Cook for 2 hours. Remove the ribs, wrap them in foil and place them back in the smoker for another 2 hours. Once cooked, serve and enjoy! Makes 4 servings.

1 serving: 1070 Calories; 81 g Total Fat (36 g Mono, 7 g Poly, 20 g Sat); 275 mg Cholesterol; 24 g Carbohydrate (3 g Fibre, 17 g Sugar); 56 g Protein; 2130 mg Sodium

Smoked Pork Loin

This is a forgiving recipe, so it's a good choice to start with if you are a new to the pleasures of smoking meat. The true key here is the brine, which will add flavour and moisture to the meat while it is smoking. Use this recipe as a base and then add in any additional flavours you like.

Kosher salt	1/4 cup	60 mL
Brown sugar	1/4 cup	60 mL
Paprika	1/4 cup	60 mL
Garlic powder	2 tsp.	10 mL
Dried oregano	2 tsp.	10 mL
Water	4 cups	1 L
Pork loin (about 3 lbs., 1.5 kg)	1	1

Place the first 5 ingredients in a large pot. Bring to a boil and simmer for 5 minutes. Remove from heat, chill to room temperature and then chill until ice cold.

Marinate the pork in the brine, refrigerated, for 1 hour per pound of meat. Once the meat has been in the brine for the allotted time, remove and rinse well with cold water, then pat it dry and set aside. Discard the brine.

Preheat your smoking device to 275°F (140°C) using apple wood. Smoke the pork loin for about 90 minutes, until the internal temperature is above 145°F (63°C). Let the meat rest, covered, for 15 minutes, then slice and enjoy. Makes 6 servings.

1 serving: 320 Calories; 12 g Total Fat (6 g Mono, 1.5 g Poly, 4.5 g Sat); 150 mg Cholesterol; 3 g Carbohydrate (0 g Fibre, 2 g Sugar); 47 g Protein; 650 mg Sodium

Country-style Pork

Some find country-style pork ribs, which are generally boneless, superior to side ribs or back ribs because they are so easy to eat. Regardless of your opinion on bone-in vs. boneless, this recipe guarantees moist, tender pork with a golden glaze. You'll love the wonderful smoky taste that permeates the meat.

Barbecue sauce (try Root Beer Barbecue Sauce, p. 152)	1 cup	250 mL
Liquid honey	1/4 cup	60 mL
Soy sauce	1 tbsp.	15 mL
Chopped onion	1/2 cup	125 mL
Garlic cloves, minced (or 1/2 tsp., 2 mL, powder), optional	2	2
Country-style pork rib ends	3 lbs.	1.4 kg

For the marinade, combine the first 5 ingredients in a small bowl. Pour into a shallow dish or resealable freezer bag.

Add the ribs, turning to make sure they are well coated. Cover with plastic wrap or seal the bag. Marinate in the fridge for at least 4 hours or up to 24 hours, turning several times.

Put mesquite or hickory wood chips into your smoker box and place it on a grill on 1 side of your gas barbecue. Close the lid and heat the barbecue to medium for 15 to 20 minutes until chips are smoking. Adjust the burner under the smoker box as necessary to keep it smoking, and adjust the opposite burner to maintain a medium-low barbecue temperature. Remove the grill opposite the smoker box and place a drip pan, with 1 inch (2.5 cm) of water, directly on the heat source. Replace the grill. Drain and discard the marinade. Arrange the ribs on a greased grill over the drip pan and close the lid. Cook for 1 hour. Turn the ribs and cook for 15 to 20 minutes until tender and glazed, adding more water to the pan if necessary. Makes 6 servings.

1 serving: 440 Calories; 31 g Total Fat (13.5 g Mono, 2.5 g Poly, 11 g Sat); 110 mg Cholesterol; 9 g Carbohydrate (1 g Fibre, 6 g Sugar); 29 g Protein; 330 mg Sodium

Orange Chili-stuffed Pork Chops

A meat lover's dream—delicious, savoury bone-in pork chops stuffed with more pork! Apple wood is the obvious choice for fuel, as its fragrant, slightly sweet smoke compliments the sweet and spicy glaze. Get ready to impress at your next dinner party with this standout recipe.

Canola oil	2 tsp.	10 mL
Hot Italian sausage, casing removed	3/4 lb.	340 g
Chopped onion	1 cup	250 mL
Garlic cloves, minced	2	2
Diced red pepper	1/2 cup	125 mL
Bone-in pork rib chops, about	4	4
1 1/2 inches (3.8 cm) thick, trimmed of fat		
Salt, to taste		
Pepper, to taste		
Sweet chili sauce	1/2 cup	125 mL
Grated orange zest	2 tsp.	10 mL

Heat the canola oil in a frying pan on medium-high. Add the sausage, onion and garlic, and scramble-fry until the sausage is no longer pink. Add the red pepper and scramble-fry until tender-crisp. Set the mixture aside until cool.

Cut slits horizontally in the pork chops to create pockets and fill them with stuffing, secure them with wooden picks. Sprinkle with salt and pepper.

Combine the chili sauce and orange zest.

Put the wood chips into your smoker box and place it on one barbecue burner turned to high. Once the box begins to smoke, adjust the burner temperature to achieve an internal barbecue temperature of medium. Cook the chops over the unlit burner for about 25 minutes per side, brushing occasionally with the chili sauce mixture, until the internal temperature of the pork reaches 160°F (71°C). Cover with foil and let stand for 5 minutes. Remove picks before serving. Makes 4 servings.

1 serving: 640 Calories; 39 g Total Fat (18 g Mono, 4.5 g Poly, 13 g Sat); 160 mg Cholesterol; 20 g Carbohydrate (1 g Fibre, 15 g Sugar); 49 g Protein; 1140 mg Sodium

The filling an be made a day ahead, but the chops should be stuffed just before they are cooked. To find chops that are the required thickness, you may have to make a special request of your butcher.

Smoked Pork Hocks

These beauties are the quintessential ingredient for my version of Habitant pea soup (p. 50). A week in brine and a few hours in the smoker transforms the humble pork hock into a serious flavour booster. Add one to any soup or stew for fabulous, smoky depth and a savoury seasoning.

Water	1 cup	250 mL
Salt	2 tbsp.	30 mL
Brown sugar	3 tbsp.	45 mL
Freshly ground black pepper	2 tsp.	10 mL
Rosemary sprigs, chopped	2	2
Water	3 cups	750 mL
Maple syrup	1/3 cup	75 mL
Pork hocks (about 1 1/2 lbs., 680g, each)	4	4

Place the first amount of water into a small saucepan with the salt, brown sugar, pepper and rosemary. Bring the mixture to a simmer on medium heat, then let cool to room temperature. Add to a large resealable freezer bag with the remaining water and maple syrup.

Add the hocks. Squeeze out as much air as possible, and seal the bag. Place the bag into a container that will prevent any spills if the bag leaks. Place in the fridge for 7 days, flipping the bag every day to ensure even distribution of the brine. After the 7 days, remove the pork from the liquid and place it on a rack over a tray in the fridge overnight, uncovered, to create a pellicle. The next day, remove the pork from the fridge and preheat your smoking device to 250°F (120°C). Smoke, using apple wood, for 4 to 5 hours, or until the hocks are a deep, dark brown and have an internal temperature of 175°F (80°C). Ensure that both the colour and temperature requirements are met. Once done, let the hocks cool to room temperature, then wrap and refrigerate them until needed. Makes 4 hocks.

1/2 hock: 670 Calories; 49 g Total Fat (0 g Mono, 0 g Poly, 18 g Sat); 275 mg Cholesterol; 1 g Carbohydrate (0 g Fibre, 1 g Sugar); 55 g Protein; 3510 mg Sodium

Try making a smoked pork hock stock—when finished, discard the bones, but pull the meat off to garnish a delightfully rich noodle soup.

Habitant-style Pea and Smoked Pork Hock Soup

This is my take on a 400-year-old traditional soup. I've used split green peas instead of yellow, and gone with a smoked pork hock instead of the usual ham hock. The flavour of the green peas combined with the smoked pork create a beautiful bowl of comfort. Garnish simply with croutons, a bit of sliced parsley, a drizzle of olive oil and a healthy crack of black pepper.

Medium onion, peeled and cut into chunks	1	1
Celery stalks, cut into chunks	2	2
Small carrots, cut into chunks	2	2
Garlic cloves, peeled	8	8
Lard	1/4 cup	60 mL
Smoked Pork Hocks (p. 48)	2	2
Pork (or chicken) broth, or water	16 cups	4 L
Green split peas	1 lb.	454 g
Rosemary sprigs, leaves picked and chopped fine	2	2
Salt, to taste		

Pulse the onion, celery, carrot and garlic in a food processor until they resemble a coarse puree. You can mince everything by hand if you don't have a food processor.

On medium heat, melt the lard in a large, heavy-bottomed pot. Add the pureed vegetables and cook, stirring often, until just starting to caramelize, about 5 minutes. Once the vegetables are lightly browned (be sure not to burn the garlic), add the pork hocks, meat broth and split peas. Turn up the heat until the soup just starts to simmer, then turn to low and cover. Cook until the pork hocks are fork tender and the peas are cooked and have started to thicken the soup. This process can take upwards of 2 hours and will require some attention from the cook, stirring every so often and adding some water if the soup gets too thick. Once the pork hocks are tender, remove them from the pot and transfer to a plate. Wrap tightly in plastic wrap and allow to cool before picking off the meat. During this cooling time, the soup can continue to simmer on low heat. Pick the meat off of the bone in large chunks and place back into the soup to finish. Adjust the consistency with water, and season with chopped rosemary and salt to taste. Makes about 22 cups (5.5 L).

1 cup (250 mL): 230 Calories; 12 g Total Fat (0 g Mono, 0 g Poly, 4.5 g Sat); 50 mg Cholesterol; 15 g Carbohydrate (2 g Fibre, 4 g Sugar); 18 g Protein; 1130 mg Sodium

Using lard instead of vegetable oil in this recipe reinforces the richness of the smoked pork hocks. Traditionally, rendered pork fat was used for most cooking in Canada and should be back in people's homes, as it is high in monounsaturated fats and oleic acid—both better than butter.

Smoky Porchetta

In the Lazio region of Italy, porchetta is a celebrated tradition. A delicious, savoury, porky tradition. Generally, a small whole pig is de-boned, rolled up with a spice paste and roasted until juicy and crisp, then sliced and served in a sandwich. It can be a bit tricky to have it turn out perfectly, but with this recipe, it's quite simple. To keep it even easier, ask your butcher to trim the meat for you.

Head of garlic, peeled	1	1
Fresh rosemary sprigs, chopped	7	7
Fennel seeds, crushed	1 tsp.	5 mL
Black peppercorns, crushed	1 tsp.	5 mL
Red chili flakes	1 tsp.	5 mL
Extra virgin olive oil	1/4 cup	60 mL
Boneless pork belly, skinned and trimmed of any thick fat (about 3 lbs., 1.4 kg)	1	1
Boneless pork loin, trimmed of fat and connective tissue (about 3 lbs., 1.4 kg)	1	1
Salt, to taste		

To make the spice paste, mix the first 6 ingredients in a small mixing bowl until well combined. Set aside.

On a large baking sheet, lay out the pork belly and pork loin, and season liberally with salt, about 1 tsp. (5 mL) per 1 lb. (454 g) of meat.

Turn the belly fat side down and spread generously with the spice paste—most, if not all, of the paste will be necessary.

Place the pork loin in the centre of the pork belly, and roll the belly over top of it, creating a cylinder. Cut several pieces of butcher's twine and tie around the cylinder until snug and tight. Reserve at room temperature while your smoker heats.

Heat your smoking device to 160°F (71°C) using apple wood, then place the pork in. Cook until the internal temperature reaches 150°F (65°C), about 3 1/2 hours. Let meat rest for 15 minutes wrapped in aluminum foil, then slice across the cylinder into 1/8 inch (3 mm) slices and serve. Makes 10 servings.

1 serving: 940 Calories; 83 g Total Fat (40 g Mono, 9 g Poly, 29 g Sat); 190 mg Cholesterol; 2 g Carbohydrate (0 g Fibre, 0 g Sugar); 44 g Protein; 135 mg Sodium

One additional step is to get a bit of a sear on the outside of the porchetta. I use my charcoal barbecue that has been heavily stoked to quickly roast the outside of the meat over direct heat, after it has rested.

Maple-smoked Pork Loin

This very versatile preparation works at home as a main meat dish, served with roasted potatoes, sauerkraut and mustard, or sliced into thin steaks and quickly seared with eggs for breakfast. It's our version of Canadian bacon.

Water	3 cups	750 mL
Maple syrup	1/3 cup	75 mL
Lemon, halved and juiced, fruit reserved	1	1
Garlic cloves, smashed	4	4
Salt	1/4 cup	60 mL
Chili flakes	1/4 tsp.	1 mL
Fenugreek seed	1/4 tsp.	1 mL
Black peppercorns	1/2 tsp.	2 mL
Mustard seeds	1 tsp.	5 mL
Water	3 cups	750 mL
Pork loin, trimmed, with a 1/3 inch (1 cm) layer of fat left on	2 1/4 lbs.	1 kg
Maple syrup	2 tsp.	10 mL

For the brine, in a large saucepot, add the first amounts of water and maple syrup, lemon (juice and fruit), garlic, salt and spices and slowly bring to a boil. Remove from the heat and steep for 1 hour.

Add the remaining water, pour into a suitable container and chill until cold.

Once cold, pour into a resealable freezer bag and add the pork. Seal the bag and place into a container that will hold its volume in case of a spill. Let stand for 72 hours, flipping over half way through.

After the 72 hours, remove the pork from the brine and pat dry with a paper towel. Preheat your smoking device to 195°F (90°C) using maple wood.

Rub the pork with the second amount of maple syrup and insert a probe thermometer into the thickest part of the meat. Smoke until the internal temperature of the pork reaches 140°F (60°C), about 3 1/4 hours. Makes 4 servings as a main course.

1 serving: 360 Calories; 14 g Total Fat (6 g Mono, 1.5 g Poly, 4.5 g Sat); 165 mg Cholesterol; 5 g Carbohydrate (0 g Fibre, 4 g Sugar); 52 g Protein; 1290 mg Sodium

 Fenugreek is a spice commonly used in South Asian dishes. It has a distinct maple aroma and pairs wonderfully with maple syrup.

Cider-glazed Pork Back Ribs

Back ribs make a fantastic meal. They generally have a good amount of meat on the bones and absorb smoke flavour very well. They are a bit leaner than other cuts, such as side ribs, so a bit of extra attention is needed to ensure they cook slowly and stay moist and delicious.

Slabs pork back ribs (about 4 lbs., 1.8 kg, total)	2	2
Coriander seed	1 tsp.	5 mL
Cinnamon stick (about 2 inch, 5 cm, long)	1	1
"Points" of a star anise	2	2
Sea salt	3 tbsp.	45 mL
Brown sugar	3 tbsp.	45 mL
Freshly ground black pepper	1/4 tsp.	1 mL
Onion powder	1 tsp.	5 mL
Garlic powder	1/2 tsp.	2 mL
Mild paprika	1 tbsp.	15 mL
Cayenne pepper	1/4 tsp.	1 mL
Dried oregano	1/4 tsp.	1 mL
Yellow mustard	2 tbsp.	30 mL
Dry apple cider	2/3 cup	150 mL

Sweet Onion and Apple Cider Barbecue
   Sauce (p. 150), as needed

Place the ribs flesh side up on a cutting board and trim off any loose bits of meat so they appear neat and tidy. Repeat for the other slab.

Grind the coriander, cinnamon, and star anise into a powder. Combine with the next 8 ingredients in a bowl and mix well.

Slather the mustard all over both sides of the ribs, then coat liberally with the rub (you won't need all the rub).

Pour the cider into a spray bottle and set aside.

Place the ribs on a smoker rack and preheat your smoking device to 225°F (110°C) using apple wood. Cook for about 5 hours, and spray with cider every 30 minutes after 2 hours of cooking.

Check for tenderness at 4 hours. Once the ribs are ready, glaze them with barbecue sauce and cook for another 30 minutes. Glaze one last time, then cut ribs between the bones and serve. Makes 4 servings.

1 serving: 1470 Calories; 112 g Total Fat (52 g Mono, 9 g Poly, 40 g Sat); 365 mg Cholesterol; 32 g Carbohydrate (2 g Fibre, 24 g Sugar); 74 g Protein; 5500 mg Sodium

Alder Wood Smoked Bacon

Making your own bacon is possibly the most satisfying smoking experience. Turning a few ingredients into what some consider the pinnacle of all things cooking is actually very simple—it just requires a bit of patience and some technique. Enjoy this bacon in your favourite preparations or on its own with a bit of hot mustard.

Water	4 cups	1 L
Salt	1 1/2 tbsp.	22 mL
Brown sugar	2 1/2 tbsp.	37 mL
Molasses	1 tbsp.	15 mL
Garlic cloves, minced	3	3
Maple syrup	1/4 cup	60 mL
Coarse cracked black pepper, to taste		
Pork belly	1 1/2 lbs.	1.1 kg

Combine the water, salt, brown sugar, molasses, garlic and maple syrup in a resealable freezer bag. Seal the bag and shake it to evenly distribute the ingredients.

Add the pork belly. Squeeze as much air as possible out of the bag, then seal it and place it in a container that will catch spills if the bag leaks. Refrigerate for 72 hours, flipping the bag after 36 hours to ensure the brine is evenly distributed.

After 72 hours, lightly rinse the pork and dry well with paper towel. Place it on a rack over a tray and refrigerate overnight, uncovered.

To cook, preheat your smoking device to 210°F (100°C) using alder wood. Rub the belly with maple syrup, and generously coat the meat side with pepper. Smoke until the internal temperature reaches 160°F (71°C), about 4 hours. Cool to room temperature, then refrigerate for at least 4 hours.

To serve, slice the meat into 1/4 inch (6 mm) slices, careful to cut against the grain (if your bacon has a rind, remove it before slicing, and save it for a smoky infusion to baked beans). Lay your bacon slices in an unheated cast iron skillet and turn the heat to medium. Gently cook the bacon until it is nicely caramelized on both sides. Makes the equivalent of 2 packages of bacon (about 30 strips).

1 strip: 120 Calories; 12 g Total Fat (6 g Mono, 1.5 g Poly, 4.5 g Sat); 15 mg Cholesterol; 2 g Carbohydrate (0 g Fibre, 2 g Sugar); 2 g Protein; 85 mg Sodium

Try slicing some extra thick pieces for the best BLT you will ever eat!

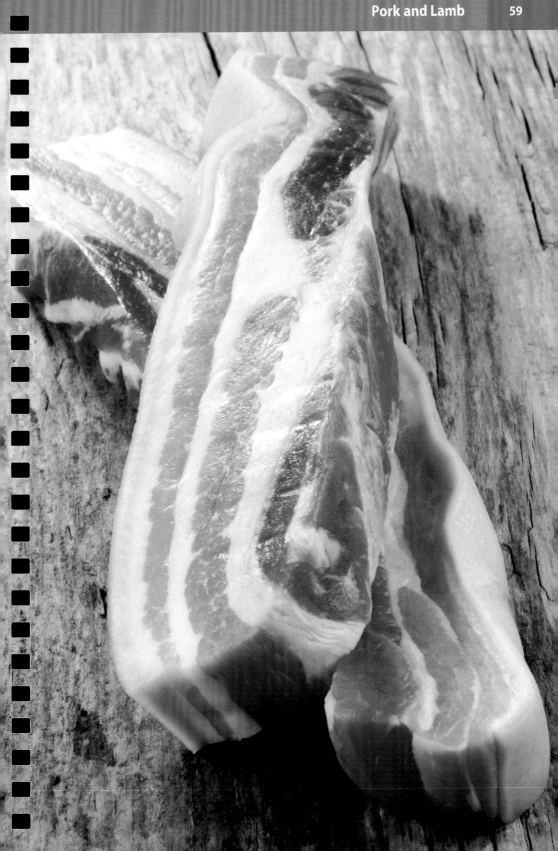

Smoked Venison Sausage

Either smoked cold or hot, these game-based sausages use regular (not lean) ground pork to keep them moist.

Juniper berries	2	2
Black peppercorns	1 tsp.	5 mL
Clove	1	1
Salt	1 1/2 tbsp.	22 mL
Brown sugar	1 tbsp.	15 mL
Ground venison, well chilled	1 3/4 lbs.	780 g
Ground pork, well chilled	1 3/4 lbs.	780 g
Garlic cloves, chopped	3	3
Bundle of hog casings (32 to 35 mm), soaked in cold water	1	1

Grind first 3 ingredients in a spice grinder into a fine powder. Mix the ground spices with the salt and brown sugar in a small bowl.

Place the ground meats, spice mixture and garlic into the bowl of a stand mixer fitted with the paddle attachment. Mix on medium speed for about 2 minutes, or until all ingredients are well incorporated and the meat is sticky. Fill your sausage stuffer with the mixture and thread a length of rinsed sausage casing onto the stuffing tube. Advance the filling until it just starts to come out of the filling tube. Knot the casing and slowly advance the filling, filling the casings somewhat loosely. Twist into approximately 12 equal links. Using the tip of a sanitized sewing needle, prick each of the sausages several times and transfer to a rack over a tray, making sure they aren't touching each other. Refrigerate overnight, uncovered, to create a pellicle and to let the sausages "cure."

For cold smoking: After curing, preheat your smoking device, keeping it under 68°F (20°C), using apple wood. Place the rack of sausages into the smoker, adding a container filled with salted ice underneath the sausages to keep the environment nice and cold. Smoke for 90 minutes, then transfer immediately to the refrigerator to chill. Use in your favourite sausage recipes.

For hot smoking: After curing, preheat your smoking device to 225°F (110°C) using apple wood. Place the rack of sausages into the smoker, piercing one lengthwise with the probe of a thermometer. Smoke until the internal temperature of the sausages reads 150°F (65°C), about 2 hours. Refrigerate immediately until ready to use. To serve after smoking, let the sausages rest at room temperature for 15 minutes, then fry or grill until golden. The sausages are cooked, so brown over high heat, so as not to overcook. Makes about a twelve 4 oz. (113 g) sausages.

1 serving: *290 Calories; 7 g Total Fat (7 g Mono, 1.5 g Poly, 7 g Sat); 100 mg Cholesterol; 2 g Carbohydrate (0 g Fibre, 1 g Sugar); 26 g Protein; 960 mg Sodium*

Cold, leftover sausages make a lovely addition to your backpack on a hike, sliced and served with hot mustard.

Yogurt-marinated Lamb Shoulder

After hours in the smoker, the yogurt marinade starts to caramelize, creating a salty, sweet, rich "bark" on the outside of the lamb. Once pulled apart, the bark mingles with tender, smoky lamb shreds, delighting your tongue with small hits of intense flavour. If possible, try to find local lamb. Canadian lamb has a much more mild, grassy flavour than lamb imported from the southern hemisphere. It's worth the search!

Sea salt	1/4 cup	60 mL
Honey	1/3 cup	75 mL
Hot chili powder	1 tsp.	5 mL
Mild paprika	2 tsp.	10 mL
Ground cumin seed	1 tsp.	5 mL
Ground black pepper	1 tsp.	5 mL
Lemons, zested	2	2
Garlic cloves, finely chopped	7	7
Full-fat yogurt	2 cups	500 mL
Piece of Canadian lamb shoulder, bone in (about 5 1/4 lbs., 2.4 kg)	1	1

Line a large roasting pan with plastic wrap. Mix the first 9 ingredients in a medium mixing bowl until well combined. Using disposable gloves (if you like…I do) rub the yogurt mixture all over the lamb, and place half of the excess marinade in the plastic-lined roasting pan. Place the lamb over top of the marinade, then cover with the remaining marinade. Fold any excess plastic wrap around the lamb, then use more to cover the whole tray. The idea is to fully surround the meat with marinade. Refrigerate for 24 to 36 hours.

Preheat your smoking device to 225°F (110°C) using alder wood. Removing the excess marinade, place the meat on a smoking rack, if using, and insert a probe thermometer into the thickest part. Smoke until the internal temperature of the meat is 220°F (105°C), about 8 hours. Let the meat rest for 30 minutes, wrapped in aluminum foil.

Gently remove the bones and pull apart the meat with gloved hands or 2 forks. Mix well and serve. Makes 9 servings.

1 serving: 380 Calories; 14 g Total Fat (6 g Mono, 1.5 g Poly, 5 g Sat); 170 mg Cholesterol; 5 g Carbohydrate (0 g Fibre, 4 g Sugar); 54 g Protein; 900 mg Sodium

Freshly ground spices ALWAYS make a better meal, no matter how many or how few you are using. Keep an extra coffee grinder in your kitchen, just for culinary use.

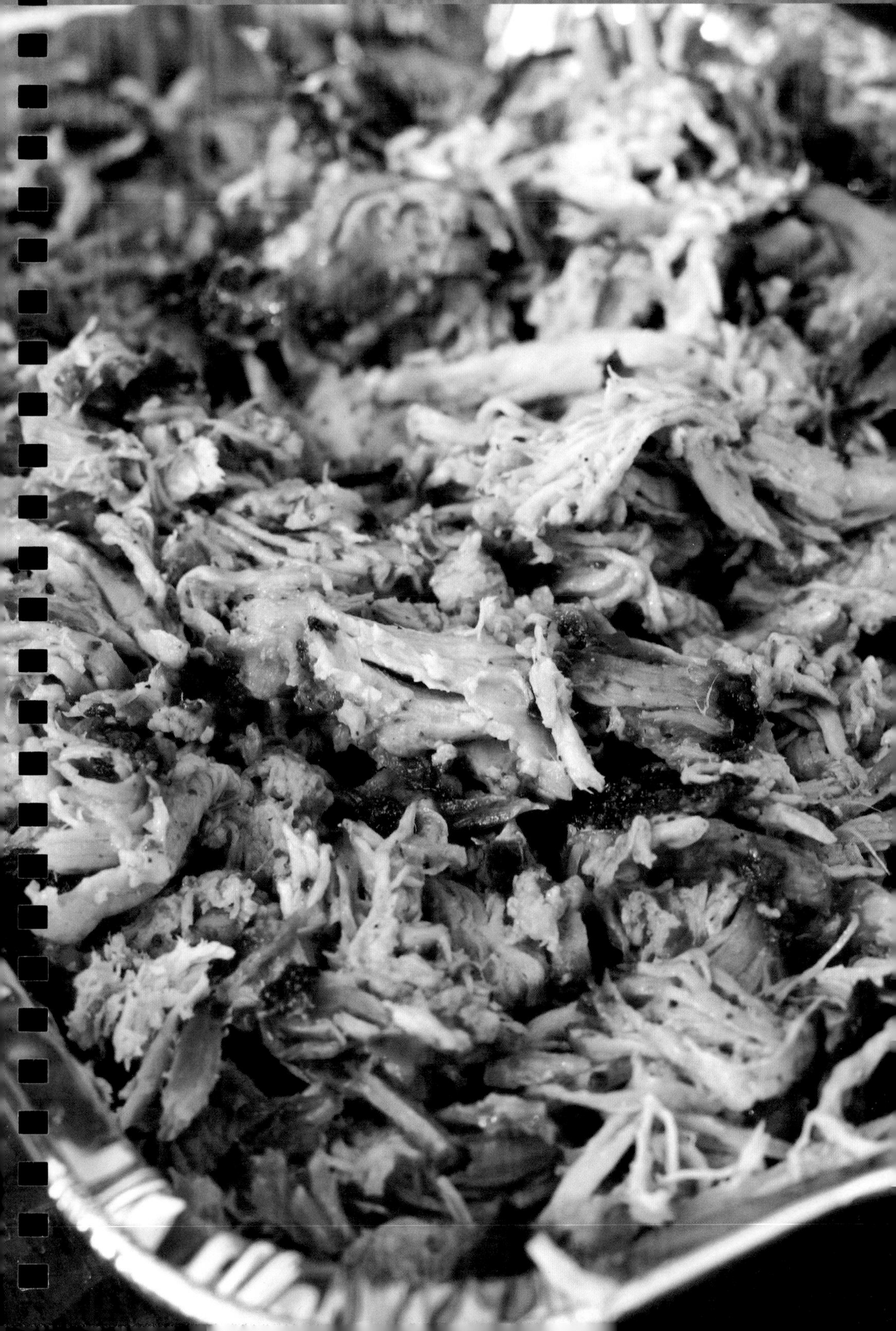

Smoked Lamb Shoulder Moussaka

This recipe has a lot of steps, but once all the prep work is done, the dish just needs baking, and it freezes well. Somewhat close to a traditional moussaka, we've substituted the ground meat sauce with our succulent, shredded lamb shoulder from the Yogurt-marinated Lamb Shoulder (p. 62) but have kept the layers of eggplant, potatoes and luscious béchamel sauce. Enjoy straight out of the oven with a simple green salad, or try it the next day, spread cold onto toast.

Japanese eggplants (about 2 1/4 lbs., 1 kg, total),peeled and sliced 1/3 inch (1 cm) thick	6	6
Sea salt	1 1/2 tsp.	7 mL
Russet potatoes	5	5
Salt	1/2 tsp.	2 mL
Olive oil	3 tbsp.	45 mL
Medium onion, minced	1	1
Garlic cloves, chopped	4	4
Strained tomatoes	4 cups	1 L
Cinnamon stick (about 3/4 inch, 2 cm, long)	1	1
Cloves	3	3
Chili flakes	1 tsp.	5 mL
Salt	1 1/2 tsp.	7 mL
Eggs, beaten	4	4
Bread crumbs	3 cups	750 mL
Smoked lamb shoulder, shredded	2 oz.	800 g
Butter	1 cup	250 mL
Homogenized milk	4 cups	1 L
All-purpose flour	1 1/3 cups	325 mL
Salt	1 tsp.	5 mL
Mozzarella cheese, grated (3/4 lb., 340 g)	3 1/3 cups	825 mL

Combine the eggplant and sea salt in a mixing bowl. Set aside for 30 minutes.

Place the potatoes in a single layer in a large pot. Sprinkle with salt and add enough water to cover by 2 inches (5 cm). Cook on medium heat until a knife can easily pierce the flesh. Drain and set aside until cool enough to handle. Peel and slice 1/3 inch (1 cm) thick. Set aside.

For the tomato sauce, add the olive oil and onions to a medium saucepan on medium heat. Cook, stirring, until the onions start to brown. Stir in the garlic, then add the tomatoes, cinnamon stick, cloves, chili flakes and next amount of salt. Simmer, covered, for about 30 minutes, stirring occasionally.

Squeeze the eggplant slices, then blot them dry on a paper towel. Line 2 baking sheets with parchment paper. Pour the beaten egg and breadcrumbs into separate shallow dishes. Dip each eggplant slice in beaten egg, then into breadcrumbs, then place onto the baking sheet. Discard any remaining egg and breadcrumbs, and bake the eggplant in 350°F (175°C) oven until browned and tender when squeezed, about 30 minutes. Do not undercook. Cool and set aside.

Stir shredded lamb into the tomato sauce and remove from heat.

For the béchamel, melt butter in a medium, heavy-bottomed saucepot on medium heat. Warm the milk in another pot, or in the microwave for a minute or so, until it reaches about 98°F (37°C). Once the butter has melted, add the flour and stir until combined. Cook, stirring, for a few minutes. Turn the heat to medium and add about 1/3 of the milk, stirring to avoid lumps. Once the mixture is simmering, stir in another 1/3 of milk. Bring the mixture back to a simmer and stir in the final 1/3. Cook, stirring to prevent burning on the bottom, for a further 5 minutes. Season with salt, cover and set aside until needed.

To assemble, arrange the potatoes on the bottom of a 9 x 13 inch (23 x 33 cm) baking dish and top with a layer of eggplant slices. Spoon the lamb sauce over top, then layer on the remaining eggplant slices and top with half of the shredded cheese. Smooth the béchamel sauce over top so it is reasonably flat and sprinkle the rest of the shredded cheese evenly over the top. Bake in 350°F (175°C) for about 1 hour, until the top is brown and bubbly, and the interior is hot. Let stand for 15 minutes or so before slicing. Serves 12.

1 serving: 750 Calories; 42 g Total Fat (13 g Mono, 3 g Poly, 21 g Sat); 200 mg Cholesterol; 61 g Carbohydrate (12 g Fibre, 7 g Sugar); 34 g Protein; 1140 mg Sodium

Tip: Using warm milk for the béchamel sauce helps to avoid serious lumps. The closer the milk is to a scald (boil) the easier it is to make a lump-free sauce.

Useful Equipment

With even simple smoking, a few pieces of specialized equipment will increase the level of deliciousness you can attain. The following are recommended items to have as part of your smoking arsenal.

Brine Injector

While not called for specifically in any recipes in this book, a brine injector is a handy tool for speeding up the brining process. Fill the needle with some brine from the recipe, then repeatedly plunge the needle into different places on the meat and inject brine directly into those muscles. For large pieces, such as bacon, the brine time can be reduced by up to 60 percent. Using a brine injector will also ensure excellent distribution of the seasonings in the brine.

Racks

Racks are very helpful tools when smoking. They are a necessity in most box type smokers, and they can also be used to transport smoked items from smoker to kitchen, and to create a pellicle in the refrigerator. The racks that Bradley smokers make tend to be pretty versatile, and I use them, even when smoking on a kettle type grill.

Brine injector

Remote Probe Thermometer

Several recipes have an internal temperature reference, both for food safety and for accurate doneness. With a thermometer that has a wired/wireless probe, you can insert the probe into the food and set the thermometer outside of the smoker, thus allowing you to always see what is happening with the food inside the smoker.

Sauce Brush

There are two basic types of sauce brush on the market—a bristled version and a silicone version. Both have pros and cons. The bristle brush (generally my preference) is excellent at transferring sauce onto ingredients, but poor quality brushes tend to lose bristles easily and don't do so well in the dishwasher. The silicone type, however, won't melt under too much heat, are pretty resilient and are dishwasher safe. But, they tend to need more strokes to apply the same amount of sauce.

Scale

After a carefully selected smoking rig, the scale is my number two priority for getting it right when smoking. In professional kitchens, EVERY ingredient is measured by weight. It is accurate, fast and guarantees a consistent result. Be sure to choose one that measures in 1 gram increments and allows you to use a variety of containers in which to weigh product—avoid the type with a proprietary bowl or container that must be used in order to use the scale properly.

Spice Grinder

"I already have a coffee grinder!" might be what you're thinking, but unless you enjoy cumin-flavoured coffee, buy an inexpensive coffee grinder to easily grind various spices into powder that can be added to a rub.

Spray Bottle

These are great for spritzing cuts of meat, fish or vegetables while smoking. For foods that require long cooking times, such as ribs or brisket, a spritz of water or flavoured liquids can ensure moist results.

Tongs

Not all tongs are created equal: aluminum can bend, plastic will melt and the locks can malfunction. Your tongs will be transporting some expensive protein that you have spent a lot of time cooking; you don't want to drop it by using inferior tongs. I recommend a sturdy, stainless steel pair with no lock.

Beer-brined Chicken

Beer can chicken is a grilling favourite, loved for its tender, flavourful meat and its cool factor at an event. That method isn't necessarily the most practical for low and slow cooking, so we've taken it upon ourselves to create a delicious, juicy beer-brined bird. Gently cooked until the point of being "just" done, it plays equally well in tacos, lettuce wraps or even just eaten off the bone.

12 1/2 oz. (355 mL) bottles of your favourite lager-style beer (not too hoppy)	3	3
Sea salt	3 tbsp.	45 mL
Brown sugar	7 1/2 tbsp.	112 mL
Garlic cloves, smashed	3	3
Freshly ground black pepper	1 1/4 tsp.	6 mL
Green onions, sliced	3	3
Ginger root, peeled and sliced	1 tbsp.	15 mL
Whole chicken (free-range if possible)	1	1

Combine the first 7 ingredients in a resealable freezer bag. Gently stir the brine until the salt has dissolved, then add in the chicken. Push out the air and seal the top of the bag. Place the bag in a pan that will catch any spills and refrigerate for 24 hours.

Remove the chicken from the brine and place on a smoking rack, if using, then over a pan. Refrigerate, uncovered, for 4 hours to create a pellicle.

Preheat your smoking device to 220°F (105°C) using alder wood. Insert a probe thermometer into the drumstick and thigh joint. Smoke until the thermometer reads 160°F (71°C), about 4 1/2 hours. Cover the cooked bird with aluminum foil and let rest for 30 minutes before carving. Makes 4 servings.

1 serving: 810 Calories; 16 g Total Fat (6 g Mono, 3.5 g Poly, 4.5 g Sat); 185 mg Cholesterol; 10 g Carbohydrate (0 g Fibre, 7 g Sugar); 141 g Protein; 1540 mg Sodium

Maple-smoked Chicken Breast

Smoked chicken breasts are great hot or cold, and they're equally great in a chicken salad. Chicken breasts are very versatile, and this recipe is another delicious way to cook them. Because chicken is so lean, the breasts will dry out if you overcook them. I think maple goes well in this dish—and it's a quintessentially Canadian ingredient we should feel justly proud of—but feel free to use honey, molasses or your favourite sweetener.

Kosher salt	1/4 cup	60 mL
Maple syrup	1/4 cup	60 mL
Cinnamon stick (3 inch, 7.5 cm, long)	1	1
Water	4 cups	1 L
Boneless chicken breasts (skin on, optional)	7	7

Place the salt, maple syrup, cinnamon stick and water in a medium pot. Bring to a boil and simmer for 10 minutes. Chill to room temperature, then refrigerate until ice cold.

Add the chicken breast and refrigerate for 1 hour per lb. (½ hour per kg) of meat.

Remove the chicken from the brine, rinse well with cold water and pat dry. Discard the brine. Preheat your smoking device to 300°F (150°C) using apple wood. Smoke the chicken for 30 minutes, maintaining a temperature of 300°F (150°C) or less, until chicken is cooked with an internal temperature of 160°F (71°C). Makes 7 servings.

1 serving: 260 Calories; 3 g Total Fat (1 g Mono, 0.5 g Poly, 1 g Sat); 135 mg Cholesterol; 1 g Carbohydrate (0 g Fibre, 1 g Sugar); 54 g Protein; 1070 mg Sodium

Chipotle and Root Beer Glazed Chicken Wings

Using smoked jalapenos (chipotle peppers) ups the level of smoky intensity in these super-addictive chicken wings. After 3 hours in your smoker, the wings take on a mahogany colour with deeply caramelized edges that are fantastic. Napkins are a must!

Salt	2 tbsp.	30 mL
Brown sugar	2 tbsp.	30 mL
Freshly ground black pepper	1/8 tsp.	0.5 mL
Chicken drumettes, wing and tips attached	4 1/2 lbs.	2 kg
Pureed chipotle peppers	2 tbsp.	30 mL
Root Beer Barbecue Sauce (p. 152), as needed		

Preheat your smoking device to 250°F (120°C) using maple wood. Mix the salt, brown sugar and black pepper together in a small bowl.

In a large mixing bowl, combine the chicken wings and chipotle pepper puree until well coated. Next, sprinkle the salt mixture (using all of it) over the coated wings and mix until evenly coated with the seasoning. Place the wings into your smoker, ensuring that they are well spaced and not touching each other. Total smoking time will be about 3 hours. After the first hour, thoroughly brush the wings with barbecue sauce, keeping in mind when basting that you are building layers of sauce. Continue to baste every 30 minutes until the wings pass the pull test (see p. 15) and are deeply caramelized. Brush one last time and serve. Makes 6 servings.

1 serving: 840 Calories; 61 g Total Fat (22 g Mono, 11 g Poly, 16 g Sat); 235 mg Cholesterol; 22 g Carbohydrate (trace Fibre, 20 g Sugar); 32 g Protein; 2810 mg Sodium

I suggest making more of these than you need. One, they are pretty delicious out of the fridge the next day on their own, but even better is pulling the meat off of the bones and putting together a quick pulled chicken sandwich to take to work and make your coworkers jealous!

Smoked Chicken Thighs

These are possibly the quickest item to prepare in the book. Make a quick seasoning, massage the thighs with it, smoke them for a couple of hours and they are ready to go. Best served alongside the Kale Caesar Salad (p. 136), they'd also be right at home chopped up into a chicken salad sandwich.

Salt	1 tbsp.	15 mL
Brown sugar	2 tbsp.	30 mL
Freshly ground black pepper	1/4 tsp.	1 mL
Paprika	1 tsp.	5 mL
Garlic powder	1/2 tsp.	2 mL
Onion powder	1/2 tsp.	2 mL
Olive oil	1 tbsp.	15 mL
Bone-in chicken thighs, skin on (about 3 lbs., 1.3 kg, total)	8	8

Mix first 7 ingredients in a large mixing bowl until a homogenous paste is achieved. Next, toss in the thighs and coat evenly with the spice paste. Preheat your smoking device to 250°F (120°C) using apple wood. Smoke the thighs for about 2 hours, until the internal temperature of the chicken reaches 160°F (71°C) and the exterior is a beautiful hazelnut brown. Serve right away, or let cool to room temperature before wrapping tightly and refrigerating. Makes 4 servings.

1 serving: 440 Calories; 34 g Total Fat (15 g Mono, 7 g Poly, 9 g Sat); 130 mg Cholesterol; 8 g Carbohydrate (0 g Fibre, 7 g Sugar); 25 g Protein; 1870 mg Sodium

There is a trick to reheating these thighs. After the smoking is finished, line a small sheet pan with parchment paper and arrange the chicken thighs on it, skin side down. Gently press the flesh side with the palm of your hand, slightly flattening the chicken. This makes the skin side of the chicken flat, ensuring even cooking of the skin. After chilling, use a cast iron pan on medium heat to gently crisp up the skin and heat the thigh through.

Apple Wood Smoked Turkey

This recipe will produce an outstanding turkey for your next holiday gathering. Brining ensures well seasoned and moist meat, and the slow smoking produces a tender, flavourful turkey. The brining is done in a cooler—most of us don't have a fridge big enough to house a turkey submerged in water!

Cold water	3 cups	750 mL
Salt	1 cup	250 mL
Granulated sugar	1 3/4 cups	425 mL
Paprika	2 tsp.	10 mL
Cinnamon stick (3 inch, 7.5 cm, long)	1	1
Black peppercorns, crushed	1 tsp.	5 mL
Lemon, juiced	1	1
Head of garlic, split	1	1
Fresh sage sprigs	6	6
Cold water	29 cups	7.25 L
Ice (buy it!)	4 1/2 lbs.	2 kg
Turkey, neck and giblets removed (about 12 lbs., 5.5 kg)	1	1

Combine the first 9 ingredients in a medium saucepan and quickly bring it to a boil, then remove it from the heat. Stir until the salt and sugar have dissolved, then refrigerate until cooled off.

In a clean, sanitized cooler, add the remaining water, ice and cooled marinade and mix well. Submerge the turkey and put the lid on the cooler. Brine for 36 hours.

Preheat your smoking device to 195°F (90°C) using apple wood. Remove the turkey from the brine and drain any excess water off the bird, then pat dry with paper towels. Place it in the smoker, and smoke until an instant read thermometer shows 160°F (71°C) in the thickest part of the breast, and the thickest part of the thigh, right next to the bone. In addition, perform a pull test (see p. 15) at the drumstick. A medium sized turkey should take about 5 hours to smoke.

Let the turkey rest, covered with aluminum foil, for 30 minutes before carving. Makes 9 servings.

1 serving: *790 Calories; 53 g Total Fat (20 g Mono, 13 g Poly, 15 g Sat); 295 mg Cholesterol; 0 g Carbohydrate (0 g Fibre, 0 g Sugar); 72 g Protein; 1430 mg Sodium*

Don't forget to make soup with those amazing smoky turkey bones!

Cinnamon Cherry Duck Breasts

The rich, complex flavours of duck are underscored with a sweet cherry sauce, with warm spicy notes provided by the red wine and cinnamon. The grilling technique ensures moist, tasty meat and crispy skin. A fantastic addition to the holiday table!

Cherry jam	1/2 cup	125 mL
Dry red wine	1/4 cup	60 mL
Red wine vinegar	1 tbsp.	15 mL
Ground cinnamon	1/4 tsp.	1 mL
Salt	1/8 tsp.	0.5 mL
Pitted sour cherries	1/2 cup	125 mL
Bone-in duck breast halves (about 14 oz., 395 g, each)	4	4
Ground cinnamon	1 tbsp.	15 mL
Brown sugar, packed	1 tsp.	5 mL
Seasoned salt	1 tsp.	5 mL

Combine the first 5 ingredients in a saucepan and simmer on medium-low for 10 minutes to blend flavours. Stir in the cherries.

Score the duck skin in a cross-hatch pattern, taking care not to cut into the meat. Combine the next 3 ingredients and rub over the skin and meat.

Fill your smoker box with cherry wood chips. Prepare the grill for indirect medium heat with a drip pan and smoker box. Cook the duck, skin side up, for 60 to 70 minutes until the internal temperature reaches 140°F (60°C) (see Note). Cover with foil and let stand for 10 minutes. Serve with the cherry mixture. Makes 4 servings.

1 serving: 640 Calories; 24 g Total Fat (6 g Mono, 3 g Poly, 9 g Sat); 305 mg Cholesterol; 32 g Carbohydrate (1 g Fibre, 28 g Sugar); 73 g Protein; 800 mg Sodium

Note: For safety reasons, pregnant women and anyone with a compromised immune system should cook their duck to medium-well doneness (170°F, 77°C).

Duck Breast Ham

This recipe was quite prevalent on menus of fine dining restaurants during the early 2000s. It's pretty straightforward to prepare, but will wow your guests with it's sophisticated look and flavour. Sliced thin and served cold, it can be paired with crisp, tart apple julienne, or some sharp cheese as a part of a charcuterie and cheese board. For best results, have your butcher clean the duck breasts.

Water	1 1/4 cups	300 mL
Salt	1/4 cup	60 mL
Granulated sugar	1 1/2 tbsp.	22 mL
Black peppercorns	5	5
Cinnamon stick (1 inch, 2.5 cm, long)	1	1
Cloves	2	2
Water	3 3/4 cups	925 mL
Maple syrup	1/4 cup	60 mL
Duck breasts (about 2 lbs., 900 g, total)	4	4

For the brine, combine the first 6 ingredients in a small saucepot on medium-high heat. Once up to a simmer, remove from heat and cool to room temperature. Stir in the remaining water and maple syrup, and place the duck breasts and the brine into a resealable freezer bag. Remove as much air as possible, seal the bag and place it into a container that can catch any spills. Refrigerate for 10 to 12 hours.

Remove the duck breasts from the brine and gently rinse them off. Pat dry with paper towels and refrigerate overnight on a rack over a sheet pan in order to create the pellicle. To cook, preheat your smoking device to 250°F (120°C), using maple wood. Smoke for 1 to 2 hours, until a horizontally inserted thermometer reads 140°F (60°C) (see Note, p. 78). Cool at room temperature, then wrap well and chill until ready to use. Makes 4 breasts.

1 serving: 730 Calories; 71 g Total Fat (34 g Mono, 9 g Poly, 24 g Sat); 135 mg Cholesterol; 2 g Carbohydrate (0 g Fibre, 2 g Sugar); 21 g Protein; 990 mg Sodium

These hams are very versatile—try some slices tossed in a summer salad of market greens, green beans, tomatoes, toasted almonds and a light lemon vinaigrette

Smoked Duck Legs

There is a classic French preparation of duck legs called confit, where lightly salted duck legs are cooked slowly in their own fat, rendering tender, flavourful meat. This is an ode to that technique, though rather than cooking the duck in it's own fat, we gently smoke it, coaxing the meat to yield the same satisfying—yet infinitely more complex—experience, with the layers of smoke flavour introduced. Serve atop some thinly sliced fried or roasted potatoes, or alongside the Braise French Lentils (p. 130).

Fennel seeds	1 tsp.	5 mL
Black peppercorns	1 tsp.	5 mL
Salt	3 tbsp.	45 mL
Granulated sugar	1/4 cup	60 mL
Garlic cloves, crushed	3	3
Duck legs (about 2 3/4 lbs., 1.25 kg, total)	4	4

First up is toasting the spices. Add the fennel seed and black peppercorns to a medium sauté pan and toast on medium heat, swirling the pan to ensure even toasting. As soon as you can smell the spices toasting, remove the pan from the heat. Let the spices cool, then coarsely grind them in a spice grinder. Combine with the salt, sugar and crushed garlic in a large mixing bowl. Mix well, then add the duck legs. Toss to evenly coat the legs with spice. Put the legs and spice mixture into a shallow baking dish, cover and refrigerate for 10 to 12 hours, best done overnight.

Rinse the duck legs and pat dry with paper towel. Preheat your smoking device to 250°F (120°C) using oak wood. Smoke for 5 to 6 hours, until the legs are a deep mahogany in colour and pass the pull test (see p. 15). Let cool to room temperature, then wrap well and refrigerate until ready to use. Makes 4 servings as an appetizer.

1 serving: 1220 Calories; 118 g Total Fat (56 g Mono, 15 g Poly, 40 g Sat); 230 mg Cholesterol; 3 g Carbohydrate (0 g Fibre, 3 g Sugar); 35 g Protein; 770 mg Sodium

Similar to the Smoked Chicken Thighs (p. 74), there is
a trick to getting nice crispy skin when reheating these duck
legs. After the smoking is finished, line a small sheet pan with
parchment paper and arrange the duck legs on it, skin side
down. Gently press the flesh side with the palm of your hand,
slightly flattening the duck. This makes the skin side of the duck
flat, ensuring even cooking of the skin. After chilling, use a cast
iron pan on medium heat to gently crisp up the skin and heat the
duck leg through.

Smoked Salmon

Not unlike all things smoked, smoked salmon began its journey into world-wide fame for one reason only—preservation. For millennia, cultures in North America and Europe have used salt and smoke to keep their catch edible through the cold winter months. The combination of low water activity inside the flesh (caused by the drying) and certain phenols and acids in the smoke acts as an antibacterial agent, which helps keep the food "shelf stable." Other compounds in the smoke also prevent the salmon's high oil content from going rancid. Preserving the fish was an extremely important development for these cultures because salmon run up the river for only a few months a year, so the people had a small window in which to harvest as much as possible.

In the Pacific Northwest, all the way up to Alaska, indigenous people harvested all five salmon species found on the west coast. The fish were cleaned, sliced into fillets and dried slowly in a wood-framed smokehouse to jerky-like in texture. Drying the fish slowly with low heat allowed the interior of the fish to dry as well; higher temperatures would have sealed the outer layer of the fish and broken down the collagen too much, resulting in a mushier finished product. The smoked fish kept the population fed until the next year's salmon run. These fillets needed to be re-hydrated in water, as they were quite dry, or gently warmed over a fire to soften the flesh of the fish and release the oils. Various First Nations cultures often prepared and preserved the salmon in different ways, so trading with another group who prepared a different product was quite common.

In the 1800s, Jewish immigrants from Russia and other parts of Eastern Europe arrived in the United Kingdom, bringing with them their smoking expertise. Fish from Scotland were cold smoked in brick kilns over the course of a few days, yielding a soft, smoky flesh. In present day, Scottish smoked salmon, still prized as a delicacy, is flavoured with salt, sugar, spices and smoke.

As time and advances in refrigeration progressed, smoked salmon has evolved as well. Generally, amounts of salt and sugar have decreased, as well as the amount of time the fish spends in the smokehouse. Indeed, we now cure and smoke purely for flavour and texture, as the need to preserve the fish is not nearly as great. A modern-day product from the Pacific coast known as "salmon candy," which is chunks of cured salmon that are hot smoked and glazed with maple or birch syrup, is absolutely delicious. Nova Scotia is also well known for "Nova Lox,"

Atlantic salmon that is lightly brined and cold smoked before being sliced and packaged to ship around the world.

All anglers living in salmon country have a responsibility to become proficient at smoking their own fish—it's extremely rewarding to turn your catch into smoked salmon that rivals what is sold at the market. Although this book provides the essentials to get you started with smoking your own salmon, I suggest using these recommendations as a guideline; experiment to find the technique you like best. Start with a cure, either a dry (salt and spices coat the fillets) or wet cure (brine). Brining is advisable for hot smoking (above 140°F, 60°C) as it keeps the fish moist at higher temperatures. Dry curing is ideal for cold smoking, as it helps with producing a more dense, full-flavoured finished product. Once cured, leave the fish to dry on a rack in either a windy place or in the refrigerator, to create the all-important pellicle. The pellicle is a thin, tacky surface that smoke likes to stick to, but it has another function with fish—it helps stop the formation of albumin on the fish's flesh. Albumin is a white protein that tends to come out of the fish if the temperature is too high, or if the pellicle has not been developed. It is unsightly, and is the moisture leaving your fish. Not desirable!

Happy smoking!

Smoked Artichoke and Lobster Dip

A classy twist on the classic artichoke dip, lobster elevates this creamy, rich preparation to a great dish to have on the table at a New Year's Eve party, or at a memorable brunch. An east coast colleague of mine's mother always serves her seafood dips with Triscuits —I whole heartedly embrace this suggestion!

14 oz. (398 mL) can of artichokes, drained	1	1
Frozen edamame beans, thawed	1/2 cup	125 mL
Cream cheese	3/4 cup	175 mL
Mayonnaise	1/4 cup	60 mL
Mozzarella cheese, shredded	3/4 cup	175 mL
Sliced chives	2 tbsp.	30 mL
Freshly ground black pepper	1/8 tsp.	0.5 mL
Lemon, juiced	1/2	1/2
Lobster meat, cooked and chopped	2 1/4 oz.	65 g
Hot sauce, to taste		

Preheat your smoking device to 200°F (95°C) using alder wood. Smoke the artichokes for about 20 minutes, very lightly smoking them. Set aside to cool.

Place the cooled artichokes and edamame in a food processor and pulse until coarsely chopped.

In an electric mixer, beat the cream cheese until softened and smooth in appearance. Add the mayonnaise and beat slowly until well incorporated.

Use a spatula to fold in the next 5 ingredients, and add as much or as little hot sauce as you feel good about. Spoon the dip into an ovenproof dish and bake in 375°F (190°C) oven until bubbling and brown, about 20 minutes. Makes 6 servings as an appetizer.

1 serving: 220 Calories; 18 g Total Fat (4 g Mono, 2 g Poly, 7 g Sat); 55 mg Cholesterol; 6 g Carbohydrate (1 g Fibre, 2 g Sugar); 8 g Protein; 400 mg Sodium

Herb-smoked Mussel Bruschetta

I've taken inspiration from two former colleagues for this dish: one being an Italian chef who showed me the right way to make bruschetta, and the other a highly regarded chef who served me an amazing smoked mussel dish. For my amalgamation, the mussels are hot smoked over charcoal, tomato vines and rosemary, mixed with fresh summer ingredients and heaped over garlicky, charred bread.

Roma tomatoes, diced	4	4
Zucchini, sliced 1/4 inch (3 mm) thick	1/2	1/2
Garlic cloves, peeled and smashed	2	2
Extra virgin olive oil	1/4 cup	60 mL
Salt	1/4 tsp.	1 mL
Bunch of fresh rosemary	8	8
Fresh tomato vines	8 cups	2 L
Fresh mussels, rinsed and scrubbed	2 lbs.	900 g
Italian parsley, chopped	2 tbsp.	30 mL
Sliced chives	1 tbsp.	15 mL
Thick slices of country bread	6	6
Garlic clove	1	1

Combine the tomatoes, zucchini, garlic, olive oil and salt in a mixing bowl until well mixed. Cover and let stand for about 30 minutes.

Fill a chimney starter with charcoal and set it alight. Once the charcoal has stopped flaming and is glowing red hot, pour it into your barbecue. Carefully (don't get burned!) and quickly place the rosemary and tomato vines onto the charcoal, then slide the grill into place. Lay the mussels on the grill and close the barbecue lid. Smoke for about 5 minutes; the mussels should have opened up—if they haven't, continue cooking until they have. Transfer the mussels to a stainless steel bowl, and cover the bowl with plastic wrap.

Remove the smashed garlic cloves from the tomato mixture. Once the mussels have cooled enough to handle, remove the meat from the shells and add to the tomato mixture. Pour any liquid that has accumulated in the mussel bowl into the tomatoes as well.

Using the residual heat from your barbecue, toast the bread until lightly charred, and rub both sides with the garlic clove.

Add the herbs to the mussel and tomato mixture and mix well.

Cut the slices of toast in half and arrange on a platter, then distribute the mussel salad and juices over top. Serve immediately. Makes 4 servings as an appetizer.

1 serving: 420 Calories; 19 g Total Fat (11 g Mono, 3 g Poly, 3 g Sat); 65 mg Cholesterol; 30 g Carbohydrate (2 g Fibre, 2 g Sugar); 31 g Protein; 970 mg Sodium

Cold-smoked Sockeye Salmon

Crafting your own cold-smoked lox is a very satisfying experience. The recipe is very simple, and the flavours used are just a guideline. Add or remove ingredients to your liking. Dill? Lemon zest? Even hot peppers are amazing in this application. Have your friendly neighbourhood fishmonger get your fish ready for smoking (remove the bones and clean the fillets up nicely) and take care to keep your smoker below 68°F (20°C)!

Sea salt	3/4 cup	175 mL
Granulated sugar	1 1/3 cups	325 mL
Garlic cloves	4	4
Green onions, finely sliced	8	8
Italian flat-leaved parsley, chopped	1/2 cup	125 mL
Sockeye salmon fillets, skin on, bones removed (about 1.4 kg each)	2	2

Mix the sea salt, sugar, garlic, green onion and parsley in a medium mixing bowl until well combined.

In a clean, non-reactive dish large enough to hold the fish, place a thick layer of the salt mixture, followed by the salmon, skin side down. Spread the remaining cure over the fish, ensuring nice, even coverage. Cover the dish with plastic wrap, then place a baking tray on top of the fish. Add some weight to the tray—4 or 5 cans of soup will do the trick—to help draw the moisture out of the fish. In about 24 hours, check the fish to see if it is cured. It will be firm to the touch at its thickest point. If not, check again in a few more hours, until it is firm.

Rinse the fish until all traces of the cure are gone. Pat dry and refrigerate for another 12 hours, to form a pellicle.

To start a cold smoke, set up your smoking device using alder wood, keeping the temperature below 68°F (20°C). Smoke the fish for 3 hours, monitoring the temperature frequently (see Tip). Refrigerate promptly after smoking. The salmon will keep for only 5 days in the fridge, but it freezes well. Serve as an appetizer, thinly sliced with the classic garnish of sour cream, capers and thinly sliced red onions. Makes 20 servings.

1 serving: 210 Calories; 9 g Total Fat (3 g Mono, 3.5 g Poly, 1.5 g Sat); 75 mg Cholesterol; 2 g Carbohydrate (0 g Fibre, 2 g Sugar); 28 g Protein; 700 mg Sodium

Tip: Adding bowls of salted ice to the smoker can help keep the temperature low. As well, try to pick a cool day—it will be much easier to keep the smoke cool than on a super hot summer day.

Citrus-cured Smoked Albacore Tuna

Albacore that has been frozen at sea is a wonderful fish to work with; it's sustainable, has great value, soft buttery texture and outstanding flavour. Cured with fresh citrus and soy sauce, it marries well with the light alder smoke, and will impress guests when sliced in sashimi style pieces and served simply with dried Japanese chili and soy sauce.

Lemon	1	1
Lime	1	1
Orange	1	1
Freshly ground black pepper	1/4 tsp	1 mL
Water	8 cups	2 L
Salt	1 tbsp.	15 mL
Brown sugar	1 1/2 tbsp.	22 mL
Soy sauce	6 tbsp.	90 mL
Albacore tuna loin (about 2 1/4 lbs., 1 kg)	1	1

Zest the citrus fruits and place the zest into an extra-large resealable freezer bag or sealable container large enough to hold the fish. Combine the next 5 ingredients and add to the bag. Add the fish, seal the bag and give it a gentle shake to distribute the marinade evenly. Place the bag in a roasting pan (to avoid any mess should the bag break) and cure in the fridge for 3 days.

Remove the tuna from the marinade and place it on a suitable rack in preparation for smoking. Refrigerate overnight to develop a pellicle.

To smoke, start burning a small amount of alder in your smoking device, aiming to keep the temperature of the unit no higher than 68°F (20°C). Smoke the tuna for 1 hour, keeping the temperature below 68°F (20°C). Immediately refrigerate the tuna. The fish is ready for slicing after 2 hours or more in the fridge. Makes 12 servings as an appetizer.

1 serving: 130 Calories; 4 g Total Fat (1.5 g Mono, 1 g Poly, 1 g Sat); 30 mg Cholesterol; 1 g Carbohydrate (0 g Fibre, trace Sugar); 20 g Protein; 280 mg Sodium

Use a very sharp knife on very cold fish to ensure clean, beautiful slices of tuna. You've worked hard getting this fish prepared to this stage; honour your work with a sharp knife.

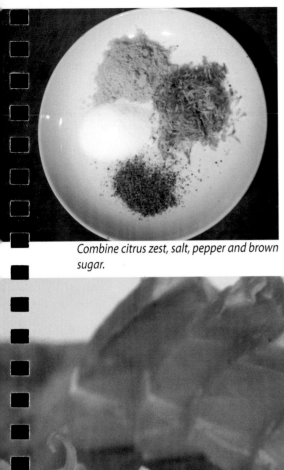

Combine citrus zest, salt, pepper and brown sugar.

Refrigerate, uncovered, overnight.

Slice and serve.

Cedar Plank Salmon

Cedar plank salmon is a classic for a reason—it's a real crowd pleaser! This version uses two other distinctly Canadian ingredients to enhance the flavour of the salmon—maple syrup and rye whisky. Try it as an addition to our Kale Caesar Salad (p. 136).

Cedar planks (see Note)	2	2
Canadian whisky (rye)	1 cup	250 mL
Maple syrup	1/2 cup	125 mL
Soy sauce	1/3 cup	75 mL
Olive oil	1/4 cup	60 mL
Parsley flakes	1/4 cup	60 mL
Sweet (or regular) chili sauce	3 tbsp.	45 mL
Pepper	1 tsp.	5 mL
Salmon fillets (about 4 oz., 113 g, each), or side of salmon (about 2 lbs., 900 g), skin removed, cut into 8 equal pieces	8	8

Place the cedar planks in a large container and add enough water to cover. Place something heavy on the planks to keep them submerged (heavy cans work well) and soak for at least 6 hours or overnight.

For the marinade, combine the next 7 ingredients in a medium bowl. Place the salmon in a large shallow baking dish and pour the marinade over top. Turn the fish until coated. Cover with plastic wrap and refrigerate for at least 30 minutes, turning occasionally. Drain and discard the marinade. Preheat your barbecue to medium-low. Place the salmon on the cedar planks on an ungreased grill and close the lid. Cook for 15 to 30 minutes, until salmon flakes easily when tested with a fork. Makes 8 servings.

1 serving: 200 Calories; 8 g Total Fat (3 g Mono, 3 g Poly, 1 g Sat); 60 mg Cholesterol; 3 g Carbohydrate (0 g Fibre, 3 g Sugar); 23 g Protein; 170 mg Sodium

Note: Cedar planks specifically designed for barbecuing can be purchased in the meat department of large grocery stores. Or use an untreated western red cedar plank found in building supply stores. Never use a treated cedar plank. Planks should be about 16 x 6 x 1/2 inches (40 x 15 x 1.2 cm) and are good for 1 use each.

Smoked Fennel Trout

If you have the opportunity to use a trout freshly caught at your favourite fishing hole, it will greatly enhance the flavour of this dish. The earthy taste of wild trout combined with the sweet anise aroma of the fennel seed pair well with eggs and hollandaise for a decadent brunch dish.

Water	4 cups	1 L
Chopped onion	1 cup	250 mL
Coarse salt	2/3 cup	150 mL
Fennel seed, crushed	2 tbsp.	30 mL
Garlic cloves, minced	2	2
Whole rainbow trout (about 7 oz., 200 g, each), pan-ready	4	4
Fennel seed, crushed	2 tsp.	10 mL
Lemon slices, halved	8	8

Stir the first 5 ingredients in a 9 × 13 inch (23 × 33 cm) baking dish until the salt dissolves. Add the fish and cover with plastic wrap. Set a cutting board over top and use a weight to keep the fish submerged. Chill for 1 hour. Rinse the fish and pat it dry, discarding the brine.

Sprinkle the second amount of fennel seed in the fish cavity and fill with lemon slices.

Preheat your smoking device to 250°F (120°C) using alder wood. Smoke for approximately 15 minutes, or until the flesh flakes easily when tested with a fork. Makes 8 servings.

1 serving: 140 Calories; 4 g Total Fat (1.5 g Mono, 1.5 g Poly, 1 g Sat); 65 mg Cholesterol; 2 g Carbohydrate (trace Fibre, 0 g Sugar); 23 g Protein; 880 mg Sodium

Immersing fish in a higher-concentration salt solution allows the fish to absorb the liquid and to be infused by the flavours it contains. When cooked, brined fish retains much of this moisture.

Smoked Dungeness Crab Spaghetti

The west coast is home to the celebrated Dungeness crab, with its sweet, briny meat filling its ample shell. This dish is perfect on a hot summer day, only requiring you to cook noodles, then toss with the rest of the ingredients, like a salad. Picking the meat out of the crabs is slightly tedious work, but is worth every moment once the job is done and the food is on the table. Ask your fishmonger to kill, clean and crack the crabs for you.

Dungeness crabs (about 2 1/2 lbs., 1 kg, each)	2	2
Extra virgin olive oil	1/3 cup	75 mL
Ripe Roma tomatoes	3	3
Garlic cloves, smashed	3	3
Sprigs of basil	2	2
Medium zucchini	1	1
Chili flakes, to taste		
Sea salt, to taste		
Spaghetti	1 lb.	454 g
Sprig of basil	1	1

Preheat your smoking device to 175°F (80°C) using alder wood, and smoke the crab for about 4 hours. Check doneness by cracking open a claw—if the meat comes out easily, it's ready. Once cooked, crack the claws, legs and bodies, and pick out all the meat, being careful not to get any shells in the meat. Set aside.

In a large bowl, gently combine the next 7 ingredients. Cover with plastic wrap, and let marinate for about 1 hour (use the time to clean your crab!). Remove and discard the basil sprig and garlic cloves.

Cook the spaghetti in a large pot of boiling, salty water until al dente—use the manufacturer's instructions as a gauge, but taste every so often and cook until you like the doneness.

Meanwhile, add the crab meat to the tomato mixture and stir. Add the drained pasta and toss until well combined, then sprinkle with the torn leaves of the last sprig of basil. Taste for salt, then serve. Makes 4 servings.

*1 **serving**: 690 Calories; 21 g Total Fat (14 g Mono, 3 g Poly, 3 g Sat); 250 mg Cholesterol; 89 g Carbohydrate (5 g Fibre, 4 g Sugar); 36 g Protein; 350 mg Sodium*

If cleaning whole crabs seems like too much work, this recipe can easily be made with fresh picked crab meat instead. Spread the meat out on a tray that fits in your smoking device, and smoke at 175°F (80°C) for about 30 minutes. The crab is already cooked, so you just need to introduce a little smoke. Use your taste buds to gauge the level of smoke you prefer.

Smoky Lobster Bisque

Lobster can be seen as a very expensive ingredient to use, but not so if you use ALL of it. A pinch or two of curry powder is a wonderful addition to this creamy, rich and warming soup. I love it with a bit of chopped cilantro, roasted pumpkin seeds and toasted country bread.

Olive oil	1 tbsp.	15 mL
Lobster bodies (about 2 1/4 lbs., 1 kg, each), torn into pieces	2	2
Onion, diced into 3/4 inch (2 cm) pieces	1	1
Carrot, peeled and sliced into 3/4 inch (2 cm) thick pieces	1	1
Celery rib, sliced into 3/4 inch (2 cm) thick pieces	1	1
Head garlic, split in half	1	1
Tomato puree	1 1/4 cups	300 mL
Tomalley saved from the lobsters		
14 oz. (398 mL) can of coconut milk	1	1
Garam masala	1 tsp.	5 mL
Cayenne pepper, sprinkle		
Butter	1/4 cup	60 mL
Flour	6 tbsp.	90 mL
Salt	2 tsp.	10 mL
Worcestershire sauce	1/8 tsp.	0.5 mL

To make the broth, heat a large, heavy-bottomed pot on medium-high. Add the olive oil, lobster meat and shells, stirring every minute for 5 minutes, until the shells start to caramelize.

Add the next 4 ingredients sauté for another 2 minutes. Add the tomato puree and cook until it cooks down and starts to colour, another 3 to 4 minutes.

Add the reserved tomalley, coconut milk, garam masala, cayenne and enough water to cover the ingredients by 2 inches (5 cm). Let the broth reach a simmer and reduce the heat to just maintain a simmer for 2 hours. Top up the broth with water if it falls below the lobster and vegetables.

After 2 hours, strain the broth through a fine-mesh strainer and set aside.

In a medium heavy-bottomed pot, heat the butter and flour on medium, stirring constantly until the mixture starts to take on a blond colour. Switch to a whisk, and add a ladle of hot lobster broth as you whisk. The soup will thicken as you are whisking— be sure to beat out any lumps that may form. Continue adding the broth in stages while whisking, waiting for the soup to return to a simmer between each stage. Once all the broth is used, gently simmer the soup for 30 minutes.

Season the finished soup with salt and Worcestershire sauce. Makes 6 servings.

1 serving: 170 Calories; 14 g Total Fat (3.5 g Mono, 0.5 g Poly, 8 g Sat); 20 mg Cholesterol; 10 g Carbohydrate (trace Fibre, 2 g Sugar); 1 g Protein; 1000 mg Sodium

Best Vegetables for Smoking

Vegetables lend themselves well to the infusion of wood smoke. Choose vegetables that have a decent water content, as when they are being smoked, they can dehydrate a touch, taking on smoke while doing so.

Cauliflower

Included in this book already in the Smoked Cauliflower Gratin (p. 108), smoked cauliflower can be a showstopper on its own. Make a paste with garlic, olive oil, curry powder and yogurt, then rub it all over the outside of a whole head of cauliflower. Smoke at 300°F (150°C) until the outside has caramelized and the flesh is tender when a knife is inserted. Slice into steaks and serve with your favourite Indian-inspired side dishes.

Corn

An example of a vegetable that smokes best in its own skin. Smoke gently, not to cook through, but to infuse with smoke. Then peel off the husk and boil, grill or sauté for some added depth at the summer table.

Eggplant

Use the technique described in the Smoked Eggplant Dip (p. 104), stopping at the peeling step, to make a great summer salad. Cut the peeled eggplant into 1 inch (2.5 cm) pieces and marinate with red wine vinegar, extra virgin olive oil, chopped garlic, sliced hot peppers and plenty of fresh basil.

The Onion Family

I like to smoke onions, garlic, shallots and leeks whole, placed on a rack below a big, slow-cooking piece of meat so its drippings infuse the vegetables with even more flavour. Once the flesh is soft when pierced with a knife, remove the dark outer layer and use the rest in your favourite recipes—try smoked garlic mashed potatoes.

Squash

Add peeled and seeded chunks of squash to a 300°F (150°C) smoker. Cook until slightly softened, and finish in a hot oven to add some caramelization. Alternatively, wrap the chunks in a foil pouch with a splash of beer and cook until very soft. Puree and add a little Parmesan cheese, then serve with roast pork.

Tomatoes

Tomatoes smoke brilliantly! I recommend halving medium sized tomatoes through the poles, sprinkling with salt, freshly cracked pepper and a few leaves of thyme and smoking below 300°F (150°C) until semi-dried, resembling a sundried tomato. Use in salads, dressings, spaghetti sauce and on toast with avocado puree.

Smoked Eggplant Dip

Traditionally, baba ganoush is made by roasting whole eggplants slowly over coals, then blending in sesame seed paste, lemon and good olive oil. This version adds even more depth by giving the eggplants a slow, oaky smoke. Great with fresh bread, raw vegetables, or even that Yogurt-marinated Lamb Shoulder a few pages back (p. 62)!

Medium Japanese eggplant	4	4
Tahini	2 tbsp.	30 mL
Lemon, juiced	1	1
Garlic clove, peeled and smashed	1	1
Ground cumin seed	1/4 tsp.	1 mL
Mild paprika	1/2 tsp.	2 mL
Extra virgin olive oil	7/8 cup	200 mL
Sea salt	1 tsp.	5 mL

Preheat your smoking device to 250°F (120°C) using oak wood. Prick the eggplants all over with a fork and place them on a smoking rack, if using. Smoke for around 4 hours, until very soft when squeezed (they should be very well cooked). Once cool, split the eggplants lengthways and scoop out the flesh.

Combine the eggplant flesh, tahini, lemon juice, garlic and spices in a food processor, occasionally scraping down sides of bowl, until smooth.

With the food processor running, slowly pour in the olive oil, creating a smooth, creamy emulsion. Season with salt. Chill for at least 1 hour, preferably overnight, before serving. Makes 2 cups (500 mL).

1/2 cup (125 mL): 570 Calories; 53 g Total Fat (40 g Mono, 5 g Poly, 8 g Sat); 0 mg Cholesterol; 28 g Carbohydrate (16 g Fibre, 11 g Sugar); 6 g Protein; 550 mg Sodium

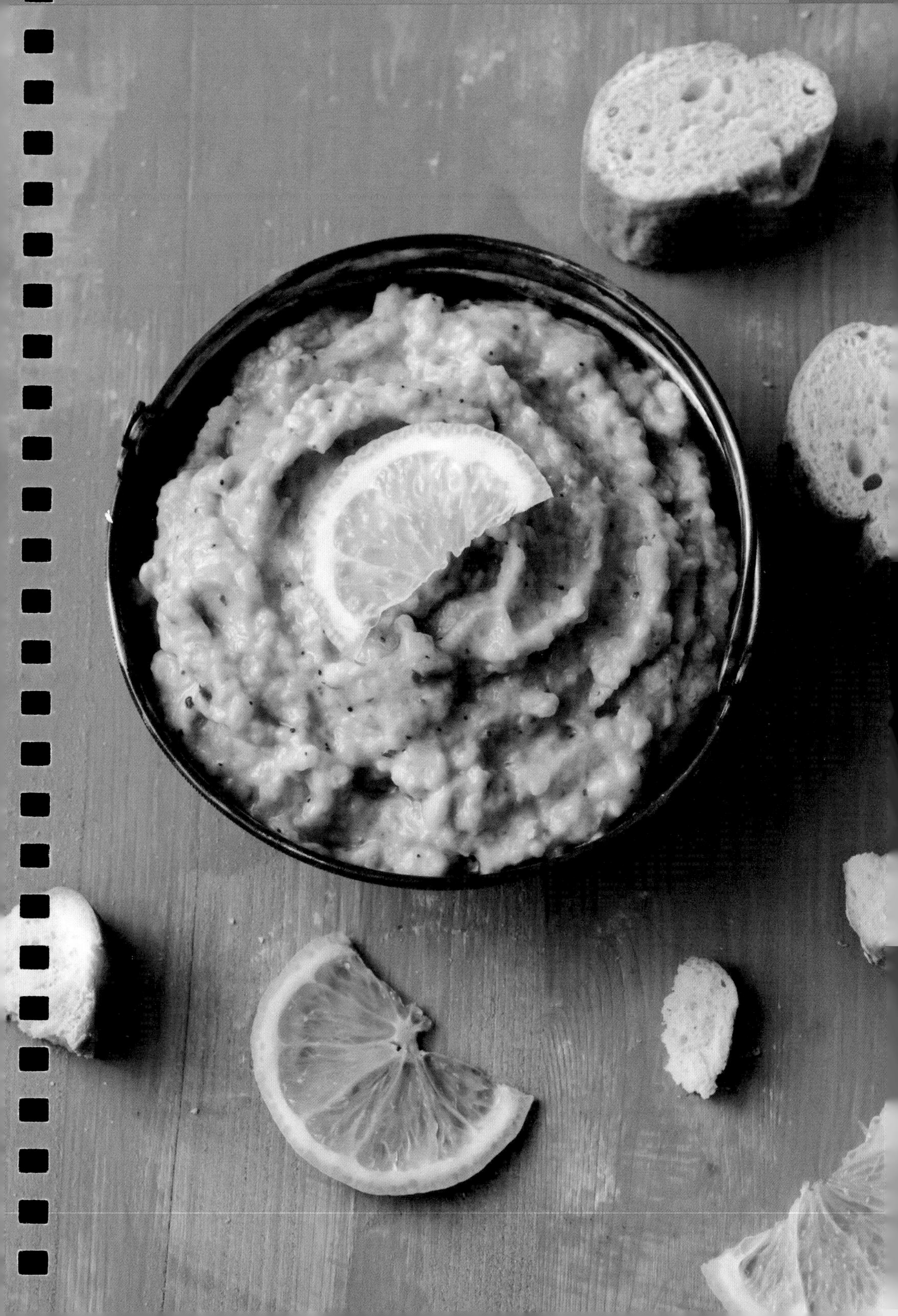

Smoked Potato Skins

After trying these comforting smoked potato skins, you may never be able to eat any other kind! Adding bacon you smoked yourself (see p. 58) makes the skins a great conversation starter next time you watch the game with friends. Be sure to have plenty of sour cream on hand for dipping.

Unpeeled medium baking potatoes	3	3
Cooking oil	2 tbsp.	30 mL
Chili powder	1 tsp.	5 mL
Ground coriander	1/2 tsp.	2 mL
Ground cumin	1/2 tsp.	2 mL
Salt	1/4 tsp.	1 mL
Pepper	1/4 tsp.	1 mL
Bacon slices, cooked crisp and crumbled	6	6
Grated Monterey Jack cheese	1/2 cup	125 mL
Grated sharp Cheddar cheese	1/2 cup	125 mL
Thinly sliced green onion	2 tbsp.	30 mL

Poke several holes randomly into the potatoes with a fork. Microwave, uncovered, on High for about 10 minutes, turning at halftime, until tender. Wrap in a tea towel and let stand for 5 minutes. Let stand, unwrapped, for another 5 minutes until cool enough to handle. Cut the potatoes lengthwise into quarters and scoop out pulp, leaving 1/4 inch (6 mm) shells. Save the pulp for another use.

Combine the next 6 ingredients in a small cup and brush over both sides of the potato shells. Preheat your smoking device to 350°F (175°C) using apple wood. Place the shells, skin side down, on the smoker rack. Smoke for 30 minutes, until the exteriors have darkened slightly.

Sprinkle the remaining 4 ingredients over top and continue smoking until the cheese has melted, another 5 to 10 minutes. Makes 12 potato skins.

1 potato skin: 170 Calories; 14 g Total Fat (6 g Mono, 1.5 g Poly, 4.5 g Sat); 25 mg Cholesterol; 7 g Carbohydrate (1 g Fibre, 1 g Sugar); 5 g Protein; 290 mg Sodium

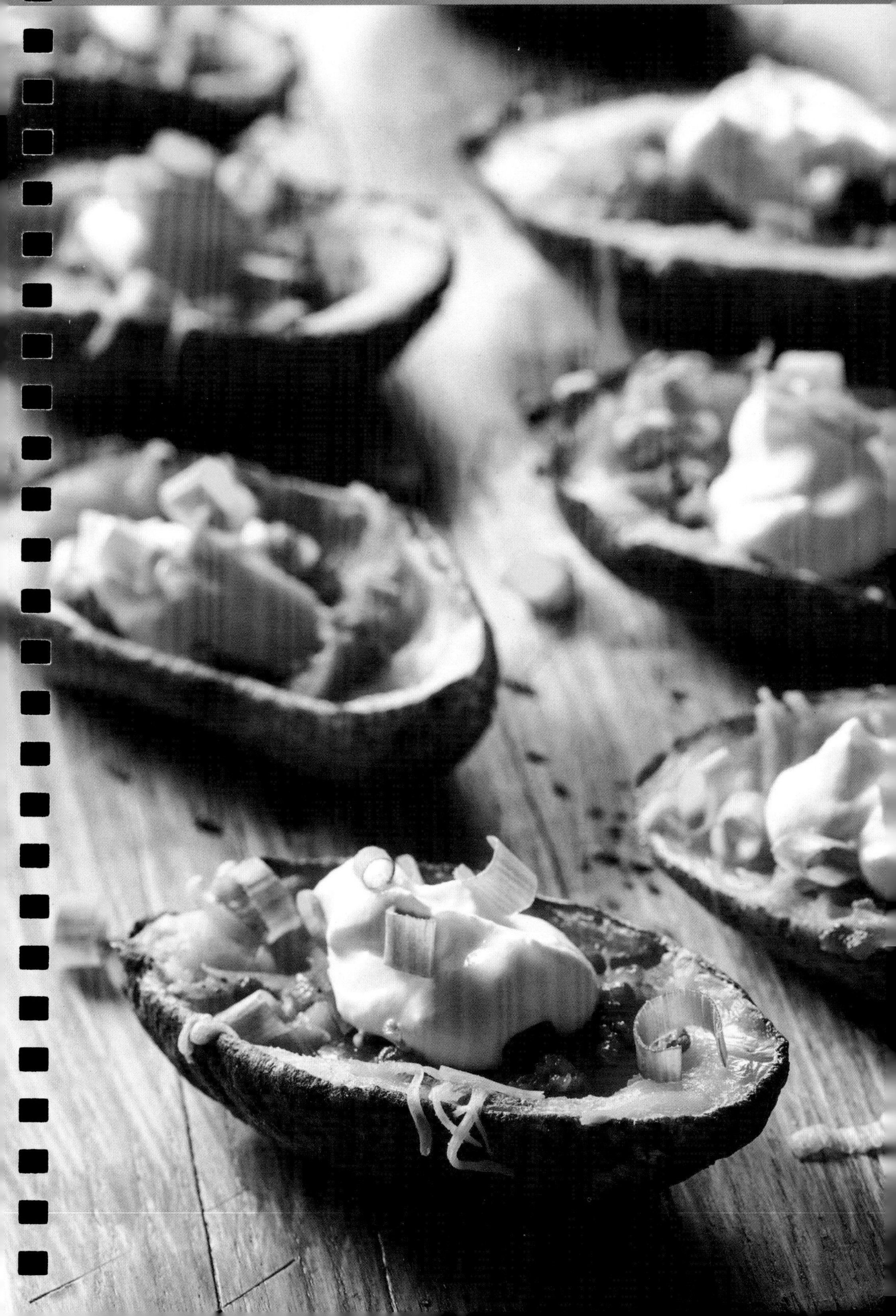

Smoked Cauliflower Gratin

Cauliflower gratin has always been a favourite of mine when dining out at a steakhouse; it is rich, creamy, and delicious. This version adds a subtle layer of smoke to the cauliflower itself, and uses the trimmings of the cauliflower stems to create a silky puree to fold through the florets.

Medium heads of cauliflower	4	4
Olive oil	1/4 cup	60 mL
Salt	1 tsp	5 mL
Half-and-half cream	2 cups	500 mL
Milk	1 2/3 cups	400 ml
Garlic cloves	3	3
Emmenthal cheese	1 cup	250 mL
Salt, to taste		
Freshly ground black pepper, to taste		
Bread crumbs	3/4 cup	175 mL
Grana padano cheese	1/2 cup	125 mL
Green onions, finely sliced	4	4

Preheat your smoking device to 300°F (150°C) using apple wood. Remove any leaves from the cauliflower, then pare the heads down to 1 1/2 inch (3.8 cm) florets, keeping all trimmings, including the stalks. Toss the florets with the olive oil and first amount of salt, and place in the smoker for 45 minutes to 1 hour, until golden brown and almost cooked.

In the meantime, chop the trimmings and stems to about 1 inch (2.5 inch) bits, then add to a medium heavy-bottomed pot along with the half-and-half cream, milk and garlic. Cook on medium heat until the cauliflower is very tender and starting to fall apart. Stir often to prevent scorching.

In a blender, puree the cooked cauliflower and its liquid in batches until very smooth, adding in the emmenthal cheese on the last batch to be pureed. In a large mixing bowl, add the puree and the smoked florets. Mix well, ensuring all of the florets are well coated with puree. Season to taste with salt and freshly ground black pepper. Pour mixture into an 8 x 12 inch (20 x 30 cm) baking dish, using a spatula to ensure the mixture has an even height. Sprinkle the bread crumbs and grana padano cheese evenly over top, then bake in 400°F (200°C) oven for 30 minutes, until the top of the gratin is well browned and the cauliflower florets are tender when a knife is inserted.

Finish the dish with the sliced green onions. Makings 10 servings as a side dish.

1 serving: 340 Calories; 17 g Total Fat (7 g Mono, 1.5 g Poly, 7 g Sat); 35 mg Cholesterol; 36 g Carbohydrate (8 g Fibre, 14 g Sugar); 18 g Protein; 570 mg Sodium

This can be made ahead up until the baking step, then refrigerated for 1 or 2 days until ready to serve. Just change the oven temperature to 350°F (175°C) and the baking time to about 1 hour.

Stuffed Summer Squash

Zucchini are made to be stuffed—try this simple stuffed squash recipe as a side dish to any of the smoked meats in this book, or even on it's own with a light green salad for lunch. Long, thin Asian eggplants also work well in this recipe.

Medium summer squash (green or yellow zucchini)	6	6
Olive oil	2 tbsp.	30 mL
Medium red onion, finely chopped	1	1
Celery stalk, diced	1	1
Ground cumin	1 tbsp.	15 mL
Fresh thyme, chopped	1/2 tbsp.	7 mL
Garlic cloves, minced	3	3
Tomato paste	1 tbsp.	15 mL
Medium tomatoes, seeded and diced	2	2
Large carrot, finely grated	1	1
Large yam, peeled and diced	1	1
Salt	1 tsp.	5 mL
Bay leaf	1	1
Smoked Gruyere cheese, grated (see p. 142)	3/4 cup	175 mL
Fresh basil, chopped	1 tbsp.	15 mL
Olive oil	2 tbsp.	30 mL

Slice the squash in half and carefully scoop out the flesh, leaving a 1/4 inch (6 mm) ring around the squash and keeping the outer skin intact. Chop the flesh on a cutting board and set aside.

Heat the olive oil in a large frying pan on medium. Add the next 4 ingredients and cook without browning for 2 to 3 minutes, stirring occasionally. Add the next 3 ingredients and cook, stirring, for 5 minutes. Add the carrots, yams, squash flesh, salt and bay leaf. Cover and simmer for about 20 minutes, stirring occasionally, until the vegetables are soft.

Discard the bay leaf. Stir in 1/2 cup (125 mL) cheese and 1/2 tbsp. (7 mL) basil. Stuff the squash shells with the vegetable mixture and sprinkle with the remaining cheese and basil. Place the shells in a casserole dish and drizzle with remaining olive oil. Pour 1 cup (250 mL) water on the bottom of the dish and bake in 400°F (200°C) oven until golden, about 40 to 45 minutes. Makes 6 servings.

1 serving: 220 Calories; 14 g Total Fat (8 g Mono, 1.5 g Poly, 4 g Sat); 15 mg Cholesterol; 49 g Carbohydrate (5 g Fibre, 7 g Sugar); 8 g Protein; 500 mg Sodium

Maple-smoked Squash

Try this stunning side for your next family gathering; your relatives will be sure to ask you for your secret. The key to this recipe is being patient when smoking the squash—low and slow is the key, as the natural sweetness will be enhanced.

Cooking oil	2 tsp.	10 mL
Medium acorn squash (about 1 1/4 lbs., 560 g, each), cut in half lengthwise and seeded	2	2
Finely chopped onion	1/4 cup	60 mL
Garlic clove, minced	1	1
Butter	4 tsp.	20 mL
Balsamic vinegar	1 1/2 tbsp.	22 mL
Blackstrap molasses	3 tbsp.	45 mL
Chili sauce	3 tbsp.	45 mL
19 oz. (540 mL) can of romano beans, rinsed and drained	1	1
Chopped pecans (or walnuts), toasted	2 tbsp.	30 mL

Preheat your smoking device to 300°F (150°C) with maple wood. Brush the oil on the squash's cut sides. Place, cut side down, on a smoking rack and cook for 30 minutes, until lightly browned and softened.

Meanwhile sauté the onion and garlic in butter in a large frying pan until the onion is soft and starting to brown. Add the vinegar, molasses and chili sauce and cook until the mixture is bubbling, then remove from heat.

Stir in the beans, mashing a few with the back of your spoon, until thick and combined with the sauce. Turn the squash so the cut side is up and spoon 1/4 of bean mixture into each squash. Close the lid and cook for about 30 minutes until tender.

Just before serving, sprinkle 1 1/2 tsp. (7 mL) pecans over the bean mixture in each squash. Makes 4 servings.

1 serving: 290 Calories; 7 g Total Fat (2.5 g Mono, 1 g Poly, 2.5 g Sat); 10 mg Cholesterol; 55 g Carbohydrate (10 g Fibre, 20 g Sugar); 8 g Protein; 210 mg Sodium

Tomato Salad with Smoked Onion Dressing

To me, the pinnacle of summer is at the end of August, when the farmers' market is packed full of so much amazing produce, highlighted with the best tomatoes one can buy. Or, if you are really fortunate, they are coming from your own garden. I like to showcase these perfect ingredients with a simple, but flavourful, dressing and some fresh basil. You won't need all the dressing, but it will keep in the fridge for up to 5 days.

Whole onions	4	4
White wine vinegar	6 tbsp.	90 mL
Granulated sugar	1 tbsp.	15 mL
Freshly ground black pepper	1/4 tsp.	1 mL
Salt	1 tsp.	5 mL
Olive oil	2/3 cup	150 mL
Fresh garden tomatoes, sliced 3/4 inch thick	2 1/4 lbs.	1 kg
Sprigs of fresh basil leaves, torn into 1 inch (2.5 cm) pieces	2	2
Coarse sea salt, such as Maldon, to taste		
Freshly ground black pepper, to taste		
Olive oil, to taste		

Preheat your smoking device to 350°F (175°C) using alder wood. Place the onions in the smoker and smoke for about 2 hours, until the onions are very soft and you feel no resistance when inserting a sharp knife into the flesh. Cool the onions in the fridge for 2 hours.

Peel the onions and put them into a food processor bowl. Puree with the white wine vinegar, sugar, pepper and salt until smooth, then slowly drizzle in the olive oil. Pour into a suitable container and refrigerate until ready to use.

To make the salad, arrange the tomato slices artfully on a platter. Drizzle as much dressing as you prefer over top of the tomatoes. Sprinkle with sea salt and pepper, and drizzle a touch more olive oil to round out the seasoning. Finally, sprinkle the torn basil over top and serve. Makes 4 servings and 2 cups (500 mL) dressing.

1 serving with 3 tbsp. (45mL) dressing: 290 Calories; 25 g Total Fat (18 g Mono, 3 g Poly, 3.5 g Sat); 0 mg Cholesterol; 15 g Carbohydrate (4 g Fibre, 9 g Sugar); 3 g Protein; 760 mg Sodium

Part of the real magic in this plate is being choosy with your tomatoes. Don't just pick red beefsteak tomatoes (even though they are delicious); find green ones, yellow ones, purple ones, big ones, small ones and ones you've never tried before. The more variety, the better for the visual impact of such a beautiful summer dish.

New Potato Salad

Smoked garlic makes this simple potato salad come alive, adding just the right amount of richness and depth to make this dish a worthy addition to any barbecue or picnic spread. Enhance the flavour even more with a sprinkle of crumbled bacon.

Heads of garlic	**2**	**2**
New potatoes	**15**	**15**
Fine salt, as needed		
Large dill pickle, coarsely chopped	**1**	**1**
Pickle juice	**1/4 cup**	**60 mL**
Lemon, juiced	**1**	**1**
Dijon mustard	**1 tsp.**	**5 mL**
Olive oil	**1 cup**	**250 mL**
Green onions, finely sliced	**4**	**4**
Coarse freshly ground black pepper, to taste		

Preheat your smoking device to 300°F (150°C) using apple wood. Smoke the garlic for about 1 hour, until tender and soft. Remove 2 large cloves and refrigerate the rest for another use.

While the garlic is smoking, give the potatoes a gentle scrub under cold running water to remove any loose dirt. Place them in a pot that fits them comfortably, preferably in one layer, and cover with about 4 inches (10 cm) of cold water. Add a generous amount of fine salt (about 1 1/2 tsp., 7 mL, of salt per 4 cups, 1 L, of water) and stir. Cook on medium heat, so they are gently simmering. They should take about 15 to 20 minutes to become tender. Check doneness with a paring knife; the tip of the blade should slide in and out easily. Once cooked, drain and set aside to cool slightly.

Next, make the dressing. Combine the next 4 ingredients in a small mixing bowl. Squash the garlic cloves with your knife until they are a fine paste and add it to the bowl. Whisk the ingredients together and slowly stream in the olive oil to create a dressing. Set aside.

Cut the potatoes in half if they are small, or quarters if they are a bit larger, and mix them well with the dressing; the potatoes should still be a touch warm and they will absorb the dressing hungrily. Set aside for 30 minutes to marinate.

Sprinkle the sliced green onions over the salad and garnish with cracked black pepper. Makes 4 servings as a side.

1 serving: 570 Calories; 54 g Total Fat (39 g Mono, 6 g Poly, 8 g Sat); 0 mg Cholesterol; 22 g Carbohydrate (2 g Fibre, 3 g Sugar); 3 g Protein; 1040 mg Sodium

Smoked Vegetable Quinoa

This light, flavourful Mediterranean-inspired dish pairs especially well with any of the smoked fish recipes in this book, or serve as a refreshing, summery accompaniment to the smoked pork side ribs.

Water	1 1/2 cups	375 mL
Salt	1/8 tsp.	0.5 mL
Quinoa, rinsed and drained	1 cup	250 mL
Chopped red pepper	1 cup	250 mL
Chopped zucchini	1 cup	250 mL
Chopped onion	1/2 cup	125 mL
Olive oil	2 tbsp.	30 mL
Fresh rosemary, chopped	1/2 tsp.	2 mL
Salt	1/2 tsp.	2 mL
Pepper	1/4 tsp.	1 mL
Cherry tomatoes	10	10
Garlic clove, minced	1	1
Balsamic vinegar	3 tbsp.	45 mL
Liquid honey	2 tbsp.	30 mL
Olive oil	1 tbsp.	15 mL

Preheat your smoking device to 350°F (175°C) using alder wood. Combine the water and salt in a large saucepan and bring to a boil. Stir in the quinoa and reduce the heat to medium-low. Simmer, covered, for about 20 minutes, without stirring, until the quinoa is tender and the liquid is absorbed. Transfer to a medium bowl and fluff with a fork. Cover to keep warm and set aside.

Meanwhile, put the next 3 ingredients into a medium bowl and drizzle with olive oil. Sprinkle with rosemary, salt and pepper and toss until the vegetables are well coated. Spread in a single layer on a greased baking sheet with sides and smoke for bout 30 minutes, until starting to brown.

Add the tomatoes and garlic and toss. Smoke for another 15 minutes, until the tomatoes are hot and the vegetables are tender-crisp. Add to the quinoa and toss lightly.

Drizzle with the remaining 3 ingredients and toss until coated. Makes about 4 cups (1 L).

1/2 cup (125 mL): 140 Calories; 6 g Total Fat (3.5 g Mono, 0.5 g Poly, 0.5 g Sat); 0 mg Cholesterol; 20 g Carbohydrate (2 g Fibre, 7 g Sugar); 3 g Protein; 150 mg Sodium

Smoked Corn Salsa

As always, the smoke introduced in this recipe takes what is already a great combination of flavours and elevates them to the next level. While great any time of the year using frozen corn, give this dish a go during the peak of corn season for a flavourful addition to the summer table.

Canola oil	1 tbsp.	15 mL
Frozen kernel corn, thawed	3 cups	750 mL
Diced tomato	2 cups	500 mL
Diced red onion	1/2 cup	125 mL
Chopped fresh cilantro	2 tbsp.	30 mL
Lime juice	2 tbsp.	30 mL
Chopped fresh parsley	1 tbsp.	15 mL
Finely chopped fresh jalapeño peppers (see Tip, below)	1 tsp.	5 mL
Garlic clove, minced	1	1
Salt	1/4 tsp.	1 mL
Pepper	1/4 tsp.	1 mL

Preheat your smoking device to 350°F (175°C) using apple wood. Mix the canola oil and corn in a medium bowl. Spread evenly on a baking sheet with sides. Smoke for about 20 minutes, until the corn has started to brown and has a gently smoked flavour when tasted. Transfer to a medium bowl and set aside to cool.

Stir in the remaining 9 ingredients and serve. Makes about 4 cups (1 L).

1/2 cup (125 mL): 75 Calories; 2 g Total Fat (1 g Mono, 0.5 g Poly, 0 g Sat); 0 mg Cholesterol; 13 g Carbohydrate (2 g Fibre, 2 g Sugar); 2 g Protein; 80 mg Sodium

Tip: Hot peppers contain capsaicin in the seeds and ribs. Removing the seeds and ribs will reduce the heat. Wear rubber gloves when handling hot peppers and don't touch your eyes. Wash your hands well afterward.

Fuel Choices

The art of smoking (it is definitely more art than science), is, well, reliant on wood smoke! Several varieties of wood are available for use, and these different woods take on different forms.

VARIETIES

Keep in mind that the notes on flavour and intensity below are purely anecdotal. If you have a bunch of seasoned oak out back, use it to smoke everything! If you have a pellet smoker, use a mix of alder, apple and mesquite. The point is, make it your own. Also experiment with branches of rosemary, tomato vines and other culinary herbs added to the fire just before you finish cooking.

Alder

With a mild, light smoke flavour and sweet finish, alder is best used with shellfish, fish, poultry and light vegetables and is abundant on the west coast.

Fruit woods

These woods, such as cherry and apple, tend to impart a mild, slightly sweet and fruity flavour. They are fantastic with poultry and pork.

Maple

Maple has a very mild flavour when used for smoking and burns extremely well. It is abundant all over Canada and is typically used with pork and poultry.

Oak

A bit stronger than the fruit woods, but certainly milder than a hickory or mesquite, oak is a very versatile wood to use. A medium amount of smokiness comes from burning oak, and it works well in combination with other woods. Oak is great used on game.

Hickory

Although not a wood native to Canada, hickory is still a popular choice for smoking here. It has a distinct, strong smoky flavour and is best used on beef or other red meats.

Mesquite

I would be remiss not to mention the state of Texas' favourite wood to smoke with. Generally burned to coals before being used, mesquite has very strongly flavoured smoke and can overpower ingredients if too much is used.

FORMS

Wood pieces

These can either be split logs, chunks of wood, or in some cases even dried twigs from a particular tree. The key thing to remember when using wood that you cut yourself or buy from a wood cutter is age. It must be "seasoned," which means left to dry for at least one year. "Green" wood can give the food a black, bitter, sooty residue on the outside. Wood chunks are the best choice for a smoker that has a separated fire box.

Pellets

Wood pellets are manufactured specifically for pellet-fed smokers. Generally, the pellets are formed with compacted saw dust left over from the milling of lumber. And, of course, they are available in various flavours from various manufacturers.

Biscuits

These are produced for biscuit-fed smokers, such as a those made by Bradley. They are normally formed with wood chips and sawdust from specific varieties of wood, then pressed into pucks, packaged and sold.

Chips

Wood chips are designed to be used in conjunction with another fuel type, be it in a foil packet on a gas grill, or sprinkled over a charcoal fire in a kettle grill. Conventional wisdom insists that wood chips must be soaked before being added to a fire, but in fact, chips that have not been soaked are best because they maintain a consistent temperature during cooking and burn at a hotter temperature, creating cleaner smoke.

Charcoal

Charcoal used to be wood—before it was pre-burned in an almost oxygen-free environment. After that pre-burn, it is almost pure carbon and burns much hotter than regular wood can. A favourite of mine for grilling, charcoal can still be a great fuel for smoking, but one needs a bit of practice regulating the fire. Stick to "natural" lump charcoal as opposed to the pressed briquettes, which contain additives that will influence the way your food tastes.

Although many First Nations people and early settlers traditionally smoked food using pine needles or wood from conifers, it is not recommended. The pitch and resin in the the conifers produce a great deal of creosote (soot) when burned and can render your food inedible.

Roasted Vegetable Mix

This hearty mixture of roasted root vegetables is a staple in my kitchen. Roasting intensifies the natural flavours of these fresh ingredients, and doesn't take long to prep. Once the vegetables are on the barbecue, there is plenty of time to leisurely prepare the rest of the meal.

Small potatoes, halved	10	10
Medium onions, quartered	3	3
Large carrots, chopped into 1 inch (2.5 cm) pieces	5	5
Yellow turnip, peeled and cut into 1 inch (2.5 cm) cubes (optional)	2 1/2 cups	625 mL
Butter	3 tbsp.	45 mL
Olive oil	1 tbsp.	15 mL
Water	1 tbsp.	15 mL
Garlic cloves, minced	2	2
Dried whole oregano	1 tsp.	5 mL
Dried thyme	1 tsp.	5 mL
Dried rosemary, crushed	1 tsp.	5 mL
Seasoned salt	1 tsp.	5 mL
Pepper, to taste		

Place the 4 ingredients in a large greased roaster or foil pan.

Melt the butter in a small saucepan on low. Stir in the remaining 8 ingredients and drizzle over the vegetables. Toss until the vegetables are well coated. Cover with the lid or foil. Preheat your gas barbecue to high. Place the roaster on an ungreased grill and turn the burner under it to low. Close the lid and cook for about 30 minutes, shaking the roaster occasionally, until heated through. Give the vegetables a good stir, then cook, with lid closed, for another 30 minutes or so, until they are tender and starting to brown. Makes 7 servings.

1 serving: 230 Calories; 7 g Total Fat (2.5 g Mono, 0.5 g Poly, 3.5 g Sat); 15 mg Cholesterol; 39 g Carbohydrate (5 g Fibre, 7 g Sugar); 4 g Protein; 420 mg Sodium

Garlic and Brown Butter Mashed Potatoes

If you haven't done much cooking with brown butter, this is a great "gateway" recipe. Nutty and rich, brown butter smells amazing and helps update the classic garlic mashed potatoes. Add a pat of our Garlic and Parsley Butter (p. 154) to the top of the mashed potato dish for a colourful garnish.

Chopped peeled potato	6 cups	1.5 L
Butter	1/4 cup	60 mL
Garlic cloves, minced	6	6
Milk	1/3 cup	75 mL
Salt	1/2 tsp.	2 mL

Pour water into a large saucepan until about 1 inch (2.5 cm) deep. Add the potato and bring to a boil. Reduce the heat to medium and boil gently, covered, for 12 to 15 minutes until tender. Drain and mash the potatoes, and cover to keep warm.

Melt the butter in a small frying pan on medium. Add the garlic and cook, stirring, for about 5 minutes until the garlic is softened and the butter has taken on a light, hazelnut brown colour and nutty aroma.

Add the milk and salt. Cook, stirring, until heated through. Stir into the potato. Makes about 4 1/2 cups (1.1 L).

1/2 cup (125 mL): 130 Calories; 5 g Total Fat (1.5 g Mono, 0 g Poly, 3.5 g Sat); 15 mg Cholesterol; 19 g Carbohydrate (2 g Fibre, 1 g Sugar); 3 g Protein; 140 mg Sodium

Whisky Baked Beans

No smoked meat feast is complete without a dish of baked beans. We've used our own Root Beer Barbecue Sauce (p. 152), as well as some smoky bourbon to round out this great dish. Canned beans remove the fuss of soaking and pre-cooking.

Bourbon	1/4 cup	60 mL
Root Beer Barbecue Sauce	1/4 cup	60 mL
Maple syrup	1/4 cup	60 mL
Apple cider vinegar	1 tbsp.	15 mL
Dry mustard	1 tbsp.	15 mL
Salt	1/4 tsp.	1 mL
Pepper	1/4 tsp.	1 mL
19 oz. (540 mL) cans of navy beans, rinsed and drained	2	2
14 oz. (398 mL) can of diced tomatoes (with juice)	1	1
Finely chopped onion	1 cup	250 mL

Combine the first 7 ingredients in a large bowl. Stir in the remaining 3 ingredients. Transfer to an ungreased 2 quart (2 L) casserole and bake, covered, in 375°F (190°C) oven for 1 hour. Bake, uncovered, for about 10 minutes more until sauce is thickened. Makes about 5 cups (1.5 L).

1/2 cup (125 mL): 110 Calories; 0.5 g Total Fat (0 g Mono, 0 g Poly, 0 g Sat); 0 mg Cholesterol; 20 g Carbohydrate (5 g Fibre, 8 g Sugar); 4 g Protein; 340 mg Sodium

Braised French Lentils

Du Puy lentils are unique in the pulse world; containing much less starch than other lentils, they don't clump together when cooking and retain their texture when cooked. They are a prized ingredient around the world—so much so that some farms in Saskatchewan have started growing an equivalent lentil, usually known as a caviar lentil. Look for them in specialty stores across the country.

Onion, peeled and cut into eighths	1	1
Small carrots, peeled and cut into 1 inch (2.5 cm) pieces	2	2
Celery stalks, cut into 1 inch (2.5 cm) pieces	2	2
Garlic cloves, peeled	4	4
Olive oil (or duck fat, if you have it)	2 tbsp.	30 mL
Meat broth (try smoked duck stock!)	3 cups	750 mL
Saskatchewan-grown caviar lentils	1 cup	250 mL
Butter	3 tbsp.	45 mL
Salt, to taste		
Freshly ground black pepper, to taste		
Spinach	2 cups	500 mL

Pulse the onion, carrot, celery and garlic in a food processor until they resemble a coarse puree (if you don't have a food processor, mince everything by hand).

Heat the olive oil in a large, heavy-bottomed pot on medium. Next, add the pureed vegetables and cook, stirring often, until just starting to take on some caramelization, about 5 minutes. Once the vegetables are lightly browned (be sure not to burn the garlic), add the meat broth and lentils. Simmer over medium-low heat until the lentils are tender and most of the liquid has evaporated, about 20 to 25 minutes. The lentils should take on the appearance of risotto.

Stir in the butter, then season with salt and freshly ground black pepper to your taste. Add the spinach, stirring until it is just wilted, and serve. Makes 5 servings.

1 serving: 260 Calories; 13 g Total Fat (6 g Mono, 1 g Poly, 5 g Sat); 20 mg Cholesterol; 28 g Carbohydrate (7 g Fibre, 4 g Sugar); 11 g Protein; 490 mg Sodium

This dish is a natural accompaniment to our Smoked Duck Legs (p. 82) and is great cooked with a smoked duck broth. I always buy whole poultry and break it down so I can cook the breasts and legs, use the bones for stock, and in the case of duck, render the fat for cooking. Ask your butcher to do all the cutting for you. To make the broth, throw the duck bones into the smoker with the breasts, then make a standard poultry stock.

Sweet Stuffed Potatoes

I love stuffed vegetables for entertaining. All of the prep work can be done ahead of time, then when it's time for dinner, just pop them in the barbecue for 15 minutes, and they're ready. They are also easy to serve—one for everyone. The smoked cream cheese pairs great with the deep flavoured sweet potatoes.

Unpeeled orange-fleshed sweet potato	1 lb.	454 g
Medium baking potatoes (about 6 oz., 170 g, each)	3	3
Smoked cream cheese (see p. 142)	1/4 cup	60 mL
Finely chopped green onion	2 tbsp.	30 mL
Sun-dried tomato pesto	2 tbsp.	30 mL
Pepper	1/8 tsp.	0.5 mL

Poke several holes randomly with a fork into each sweet potato. Microwave, uncovered, on High for about 8 minutes, turning at halftime, until tender. Wrap in a tea towel and let stand for 5 minutes. Let stand unwrapped for about 5 minutes until cool enough to handle. Cut the sweet potato in half lengthwise and scoop the pulp into a medium bowl. Discard the skin. Cover the pulp to keep it warm.

Poke several holes randomly with a fork into each potato. Microwave, uncovered, on High for about 15 minutes, turning at halftime, until tender. Wrap in a tea towel and let stand for 5 minutes. Let stand unwrapped for about 5 minutes until cool enough to handle. Cut the potatoes in half lengthwise and scoop out the pulp, leaving a 1/4 inch (6 mm) shell. Add the pulp to the sweet potato and mash.

Stir in the remaining 4 ingredients and spoon into the shells. Preheat your barbecue to medium. Place the shells on a greased warming rack in the barbecue and close the lid. Cook for about 15 minutes until lightly browned and heated through. Makes 6 stuffed potatoes.

1 serving: 200 Calories; 4.5 g Total Fat (0 g Mono, 0 g Poly, 2 g Sat); 10 mg Cholesterol; 35 g Carbohydrate (4 g Fibre, 5 g Sugar); 4 g Protein; 120 mg Sodium

Bulgur and Fresh Herb Salad

A clean, cool accompaniment to our Yogurt-marinated Lamb Shoulder (p. 62), this Mediterranean-inspired salad uses fresh herbs and lemon juice to keep things fresh and light. Garnish with chopped fresh tomatoes for a little added colour if you like.

Bulgur wheat	**1 cup**	**250 mL**
Water	**2 1/2 cups**	**625 mL**
Salt	**1/4 tsp.**	**1 mL**
Red onion, finely diced	**1/2 cup**	**125 mL**
Italian parsley, chopped	**1 1/4 cups**	**300 mL**
Mint leaves, torn	**1/3 cup**	**75 mL**
Lemon, juiced	**1**	**1**
Extra virgin olive oil	**1/3 cup**	**75 mL**
Salt	**1/2 tsp.**	**2 mL**

Combine the bulgur, water and salt in a large saucepot on medium-high heat. Bring to a boil, stirring constantly, then turn down to a simmer, cover and cook for about 10 minutes, until liquid is gone. Let stand, covered, for about 15 minutes, then fluff with a fork and transfer to a medium sized mixing bowl.

Place the chopped onion in a sieve and rinse with cold water for 2 minutes, then shake dry. Add to the bulgur along with the remaining 5 ingredients and mix well. Adjust seasoning, if necessary, and serve. Makes 6 servings as a side.

1 serving: 190 Calories; 13 g Total Fat (10 g Mono, 1 g Poly, 2 g Sat); 0 mg Cholesterol; 21 g Carbohydrate (5 g Fibre, 1 g Sugar); 4 g Protein; 240 mg Sodium

When tasting, think about the level of acidity from the lemon, the richness of the olive oil and the saltiness. If you prefer one or more of these elements in greater quantities, don't be shy to adjust them as needed.

Kale Caesar Salad

Adding some ribbons of raw kale to this Caesar salad is an easy way to introduce this superfood to your family. Kid tested and approved, serve the salad with garlic croutons and Smoked Chicken Thighs (p. 74).

Head of romaine lettuce	1	1
Medium stalk of Tuscan kale	5	5
Caesar Dressing	1 cup	250 mL
Garlic croutons	1 cup	250 mL
Small (not cherry) multicoloured tomatoes, quartered	5	5
Ripe avocado, cut into 1/2 inch (6 mm) chunks	1	1
Grana padano	1/3 cup	75 mL

Fill your clean sink with cold water. Remove any ugly outer leaves of the romaine and trim the top of the head. Split the head in half, remove the core and cut into 1 1/4 inch (3 cm) square pieces. Place all the lettuce in the water. Next, remove the rib from each leaf of kale and discard. Slice the kale into 1/4 inch (6 mm) ribbons and add to the water. Wash the greens well, and spin until dry. Transfer the greens to a large mixing bowl. Add the dressing and gently mix with your hands. Once mixed, portion onto plates and garnish with croutons, tomato and avocado. Finally, using a microplane, grate the grana padano over the top of the salad. Makes 4 servings as a starter or side.

1 serving: 770 Calories; 71 g Total Fat (45 g Mono, 13 g Poly, 10 g Sat); 50 mg Cholesterol; 27 g Carbohydrate (10 g Fibre, 5 g Sugar); 13 g Protein; 470 mg Sodium

Caesar Dressing

Garlic cloves	2	2
Capers, drained and rinsed	1 1/2 tbsp.	22 mL
Anchovy fillets, rinsed	4	4
Dijon mustard	1 tbsp.	15 mL
Lemon, juiced and zested	1	1
Large egg	1	1
Egg yolk	1	1
Canola oil	1 7/8 cups	450 mL
Olive oil	1 1/4 cups	300 mL
Freshly grated grana padano cheese	1/2 cup	125 mL
Freshly ground black pepper	1/4 tsp.	1 mL
Tabasco sauce	1/8 tsp.	0.5 mL
Worcestershire sauce	1/8 tsp.	0.5 mL

(continued on next page)

Place the first 7 ingredients in the bowl of a food processor and pulse a few times until ingredients are very lightly chopped. Turn on full speed and gently stream in the canola oil. Scrape down the sides of the bowl, then gently stream in the olive oil. Pour the dressing into a suitable storage container, and stir in the cheese, pepper, Tabasco and Worcestershire sauces. The dressing should be thick, viscous and creamy. Makes about 3 cups (750 mL).

1/2 cup (125 mL): *1070 Calories; 117 g Total Fat (76 g Mono, 23 g Poly, 14 g Sat); 80 mg Cholesterol; 2 g Carbohydrate (0 g Fibre, 0 g Sugar); 6 g Protein; 350 mg Sodium*

Simple Crunchy Coleslaw

I prefer a coleslaw dressed with a vinaigrette as opposed to mayonnaise; vinaigrette keeps it light and bright, which is key when being served with a rich, fatty meat like Smoked Pork Butt (p. 34). This coleslaw will stand up overnight in the fridge.

Small head of green cabbage, shredded (about 1 1/2 lbs., 680 g)	1	1
Medium stalks of Tuscan kale, torn into small pieces, stem removed	5	5
Medium carrots, peeled and grated	4	4
Granulated sugar	1 tbsp.	15 mL
Sea salt	1/2 tbsp.	7 mL
Apple cider vinegar	1/2 cup	125 mL
Shallots, finely sliced	2/3 cup	150 mL
Grainy Dijon mustard	2 tbsp.	30 mL
Extra virgin olive oil	1 3/4 cups	425 mL
Salt	3/4 tsp.	4 mL
Freshly ground black pepper	1/4 tsp.	1 mL

Combine the first 5 ingredients in a large mixing bowl and knead well with your hands. Squeeze the vegetables to get the juices flowing and to tenderize the cabbage. Once you feel the cabbage start to succumb to all of this mixing, let it sit for about 15 minutes.

Meanwhile, mix the dressing. Whisk the vinegar, shallots and mustard in a medium mixing bowl until well combined. Then, while whisking continuously, stream in the olive oil, creating an emulsified dressing. Add the salt and pepper and set aside.

Drain the liquid from the cabbage mixture in a colander, giving the vegetables an extra squeeze to get out as much water as you can. Place the squeezed cabbage mixture in another mixing bowl. Add the vinaigrette a few spoonfuls at a time, using just enough to lightly coat the vegetables. Allow to marinate for a few minutes, then serve. Makes 6 servings.

1 serving: 820 Calories; 76 g Total Fat (55 g Mono, 8 g Poly, 11 g Sat); 0 mg Cholesterol; 34 g Carbohydrate (5 g Fibre, 12 g Sugar); 6 g Protein; 1160 mg Sodium

I use a Japanese mandolin slicer to get the cabbage nicely shredded with minimal amount of chopping—just watch your fingers!!

Quick Pickled Cucumbers

These are fresh, crisp pickles; salty and sweet, they bring alive any rich, smoked dish. A natural fit with the Szechuan Pepper Smoked Pork Belly (p. 32), stuffed in a steamed bun with some fiery hot sauce. The pickles keep well for a few days, but will start to loose their vibrancy after 24 hours.

English cucumber, thinly sliced	1/2	1/2
Granulated sugar	1/2 tsp.	2 mL
Sea salt	1/2 tsp.	2 mL
Rice wine vinegar	1 tbsp.	15 mL

Mix the cucumber slices with sugar and salt. Let marinate for about 30 minutes at room temperature. Rinse off the cucumber slices and squeeze out any excess moisture.

Season with the vinegar. Makes 6 servings.

1 serving: 5 Calories; 0 g Total Fat (0 g Mono, 0 g Poly, 0 g Sat); 0 mg Cholesterol; 1 g Carbohydrate (0 g Fibre, 1 g Sugar); 0 g Protein; 90 mg Sodium

Add more ingredients, if you like, to suit whatever your are serving these pickles with—torn mint with lamb, for example, or thinly sliced chili peppers with a chicken dish.

Smoking Cheese

What could possibly make cheese any more delicious? Smoke, of course!
To successfully smoke different cheeses, there are a few things to consider:

Texture

The most resilient cheeses to smoke have a semi-firm texture, like a Gouda,
Cheddar or Swiss. A bit of temperature fluctuation won't melt them into
a puddle, and their medium-sharp flavour picks up the smoke flavour
well. Softer cheeses, such as ricotta, fresh mozzarella or cream cheese are
great to smoke as well, but must be wrapped in cheesecloth, or placed in
a container, as they tend to melt a bit, even at relatively low temperatures.

Fat Content

Fat tends to pick up smoke easily, so when choosing cheese to expose to
wood smoke, choose a full-fat variety; keep the light cheese for some other
use. In addition, cheeses that are by nature lower in fat (ricotta, mozzarella,
etc.) will need longer exposure to the smoke.

Timing and Temperature

Place a bowl of salted ice in your smoking device, directly under your cheese, and do your best to keep the temperature down as low as possible, so that you can keep your cheese in the smoker for a good amount of time, up to 1 hour.

Appearance

You may notice that smoked cheese at the supermarket tends to have a different appearance than ones that have been smoked at home. Namely, the smoked cheddars in the shops have a paprika based rub on the outside to indicate a colour change. Others have been professionally cold smoked for hours or even days. I assure you that 1 hour in your smoker at home will give only a slight tinge of smoke colour but a world of flavour.

Uses

The obvious use is to eat smoked cheese out of hand, which, of course, is delicious, but I encourage you to try it in recipes rather than eating it on its own. Try it in grilled cheese sandwiches, grated over pasta, in salads or on homemade pizza!

Best Cheeses for Smoking

Try Cheddar, Gruyère, Gouda, grana padano, fontina, Stilton, cream cheese, ricotta, fresh/block mozzarella, provolone and brie.

Cherry and Rye Whisky Barbecue Sauce

Although meant to accompany the Pistachio-crusted Pork Side Ribs (p. 38), this sauce goes especially well with savoury inclined pastries—try it on buttered biscuits for your next picnic.

Extra virgin olive oil	1/4 cup	60 mL
Medium onion, chopped	1	1
Garlic cloves, chopped	4	4
Fresh cherries, pitted	3 cups	750 mL
White wine vinegar	1/2 cup	125 mL
Rye whisky	1/3 cup	75 mL
Sea salt	1 tsp.	5 mL
Granulated sugar	6 tbsp.	90 mL

Heat the oil in a medium saucepot on medium. Add the onion and cook, stirring often, until softened and light brown, about 10 minutes.

Add the remaining 6 ingredients and stir until well combined. Cook until thickened, about 15 to 20 minutes. With a blender, food processor or immersion blender, blend the sauce until it is smooth. Chill immediately. Makes about 2 cups (500 mL).

1/4 cup (60 mL): 160 Calories; 7 g Total Fat (6 g Mono, 0.5 g Poly, 1 g Sat); 0 mg Cholesterol; 20 g Carbohydrate (1 g Fibre, 17 g Sugar); trace Protein; 270 mg Sodium

With this recipe, the better the whiskey, the better the sauce. Use a high quality rye and want the flavour to shine a bit more, add it at the very end of the cooking time to preserve its special characteristics.

Apricot and Mustard Barbecue Sauce

This sauce pairs best with all things pork. It's tart with a touch of spice and cuts well through the fattiness of smoked pork.

Extra virgin olive oil	3 tbsp.	45 mL
Onion, chopped	1	1
Garlic cloves, peeled and smashed	3	3
Apricots, pitted (about 23 oz., 650 g)	12	12
Brown sugar	6 tbsp.	90 mL
Apple cider vinegar	6 tbsp.	90 mL
Canadian rye	1 1/4 cups	300 mL
Freshly ground black pepper	1/4 tsp.	1 mL
Whole grain mustard	3 tbsp.	45 mL
Sea salt	3/4 tsp.	4 mL

Heat the olive oil in a large saucepot on medium and lightly brown the chopped onion and garlic. Add the apricots, brown sugar, vinegar, rye and pepper. Cook for about 20 minutes, until the sauce has thickened slightly.

Add the mustard and salt, and blend in a blender until smooth. The sauce should be somewhat thick, comparable to ketchup. Makes about 2 cups (500 mL).

1/4 cup (60 mL): 220 Calories; 6 g Total Fat (4.5 g Mono, 0 g Poly, 1 g Sat); 0 mg Cholesterol; 22 g Carbohydrate (2 g Fibre, 18 g Sugar); 1 g Protein; 280 mg Sodium.

Green Onion and Ginger Sauce

A perfect accompaniment to any smoked or grilled meat, this sauce is a take on the classic ginger sauce that is normally served beside a soy sauce chicken at a Chinese barbecue restaurant. Very quick and easy to make, it keeps for a week, as long as the vinegar is added just before serving.

Green onions, finely sliced	6	6
Ginger root, finely chopped	3 tsp.	15 mL
Sea salt	1/2 tsp.	2 mL
Canola oil	6 tbsp.	90 mL
Sesame oil	1/2 tsp	2 mL
Soy sauce	1 tbsp.	15 mL
Rice vinegar	1 tbsp.	15 mL

In a small mixing bowl, combine the green onions, ginger root, salt and both oils and stir until well combined. Add the soy sauce and mix again. Refrigerate overnight before serving, if possible.

Just prior to serving, stir in the vinegar. Makes about 2 cups (500 mL).

1/4 cup (60 mL): 100 Calories; 11 g Total Fat (6 g Mono, 3 g Poly, 1 g Sat); 0 mg Cholesterol; 1 g Carbohydrate (0 g Fibre, trace Sugar); 0 g Protein; 250 mg Sodium

Sweet Onion and Apple Cider Barbecue Sauce

The addition of some finely chopped ginger root gives this sauce the perfect amount of depth needed to compliment some smoky pork back ribs. When choosing your cider remember, the better the cider, the better the sauce.

Extra virgin olive oil	3 tbsp.	45 mL
Medium onion, chopped	1	1
Medium granny smith apple, peeled, cored and sliced	1	1
Garlic cloves, chopped	5	5
Ginger root (about 1/2 inch, 12 mm long), peeled and finely chopped	1	1
Brown sugar	1/4 cup	60 mL
Apple cider vinegar	1/2 cup	125 mL
12 1/2 oz.(355 mL) bottles of dry apple cider	2	2
Freshly ground black pepper	1/4 tsp.	1 mL
Sea salt	1 tsp.	5 mL
Worcestershire sauce	1/8 tsp.	0.5 mL

Heat the olive oil in a medium saucepot on medium. Add the onions and cook, stirring occasionally, until they begin to caramelize, about 10 minutes.

Add the apples, garlic, ginger root and brown sugar. Cook for another 5 minutes; the sugar will start melting in the pan.

Add the vinegar and cook until reduced in volume by half.

Add the last 4 ingredients and cook down by half once more. Blend the sauce with an immersion blender, food processor or blender until smooth. Taste and adjust the seasonings to your taste. Makes 2 cups (500 mL).

1/4 cup (60 mL): 130 Calories; 5 g Total Fat (4 g Mono, 0 g Poly, 1 g Sat); 0 mg Cholesterol; 14 g Carbohydrate (1 g Fibre, 9 g Sugar); trace Protein; 270 mg Sodium

Root Beer Barbecue Sauce

An integral ingredient to the Chipotle and Root Beer Glazed Chicken Wings (p. 72), this sauce has great depth and balance and is more traditional in flavour than our other sauces. The botanicals in the root beer combined with the cider vinegar give it a great sweet-and-sour flavour.

Butter, unsalted	1/4 cup	60 mL
Garlic cloves, peeled and minced	4	4
Red onion, minced	2 cups	500 mL
Ketchup	7/8 cup	200 mL
Cider vinegar	2/3 cup	150 mL
Brown sugar	6 tbsp.	90 mL
Tomato sauce	7 tbsp.	105 mL
Salt	1/2 tsp.	2 mL
Freshly ground black pepper	1/4 tsp.	1 mL
Pureed chipotle peppers	1 tbsp.	15 mL
12 1/2 oz. (355 mL) can of root beer	1	1

Heat the butter in a medium saucepan on medium-low. Add the garlic and onion and cook, stirring periodically, for about 10 minutes, until the vegetables are quite soft but have not started to colour.

Stir in the last 8 ingredients and raise the heat to medium. Simmer for 30 minutes, until thickened to the consistency of a barbecue sauce. Cool and refrigerate, covered, for up to 1 week. Makes 3 cups (750 mL).

1/4 cup (60 mL): 130 Calories; 5 g Total Fat (1 g Mono, 0 g Poly, 2.5 g Sat); 10 mg Cholesterol; 24 g Carbohydrate (1 g Fibre, 22 g Sugar); 1 g Protein; 420 mg Sodium

Try to search out a less commercial root beer. In British Columbia, two breweries (Phillips in Victoria, and Caribou in Prince George) also produce a root beer. These smaller-batch-produced root beers tend to have a more interesting and "rooty" flavour profile, which is great in this sauce.

Garlic and Parsley Butter

We use this versatile compound butter to finish the Slow-smoked Prime Rib of Beef (p. 18), but the possibilities are truly endless. It gets its bright green colour from pureeing in the parsley, rather than just chopping it.

Salted butter, softened	1 lb.	454 g
Italian parsley, leaves only, chopped coarsely	1/2 cup	125 mL
Grana padano, grated fine	1/2 cup	125 mL
Garlic cloves, peeled	6	6
Freshly ground black pepper	1/4 tsp.	1 mL

Place all the ingredients into the bowl of a food processor. Process at full speed until the chopped pieces of parsley disappear and colour the butter a bright green. This should take 1 or 2 minutes. Store the butter tightly wrapped in the fridge until ready to use. Make sure to take the butter out of the fridge before using in order to ensure proper melting. Makes just over 1 lb. (454 g).

1 tbsp. (15 mL): 110 Calories; 12 g Total Fat (3 g Mono, 0 g Poly, 8 g Sat); 30 mg Cholesterol; 0 g Carbohydrate (0 g Fibre, 0 g Sugar); trace Protein; 20 mg Sodium

The ultimate use for this preparation—garlic bread!

Conversion Chart

INGREDIENT	VOLUME	WEIGHT
All-Purpose Flour, sifted	1 tbsp./ 15 mL	8 g
	1/4 cup/ 60 mL	31 g
	1/3 cup/ 75 mL	41 g
	1/2 cup/ 125 mL	62.5 g
Breadcrumbs	1 tbsp./ 15 mL	2.5 g
	1/4 cup/ 60 mL	15 g
	1/3 cup/ 75 mL	20 g
	1/2 cup/ 125 mL	25 g
Brown Sugar	1 tbsp./ 15 mL	14 g
	1/4 cup / 60 mL	55 g
	1/3 cup/ 75 mL	63 g
	1/2 cup/ 125 mL	110 g
Butter	1 tbsp./15 mL	14 g
	1/4 cup/60 mL	56 g
	1/3 cup/ 75 mL	68 g
	1/2 cup/ 125 mL	113.5 g
Chopped Fresh Herbs	1 tbsp./15 mL	2.5 g
	1/4 cup/ 60 mL	10 g
	1/3 cup/ 75 mL	12.5 g
	1/2 cup/ 125 mL	20 g
Granulated Sugar	1 tbsp./ 15 mL	12 g
	1/4 cup/ 60 mL	50 g
	1/3 cup/ 75 mL	67 g
	1/2 cup/ 125 mL	100 g
Grated Hard Cheese	1 tbsp./ 15 mL	7.5 g
	1/4 cup/ 60 mL	25 g
	1/3 cup/ 75 mL	35 g
	1/2 cup/ 125 mL	50 g
Honey	1 tbsp./ 15 mL	21 g
	1/4 cup/ 60 mL	85 g
	1/3 cup/ 75 mL	113 g
	1/2 cup/ 125 mL	170 g
Maple Syrup	1 tbsp./ 15 mL	20.5 g
	1/4 cup/ 60 mL	82 g
	1/3 cup/ 75 mL	109 g
	1/2 cup/ 125 mL	164 g
Molasses	1 tbsp./ 15 mL	19.5 g
	1/4 cup/ 60 mL	78 g
	1/3 cup/ 75 mL	104 g
	1/2 cup/ 125 mL	156 g
Salt	1 tbsp./ 15 mL	20 g
	1/4 cup/ 60 mL	80 g
	1/3 cup/ 75 mL	100 g
	1/2 cup/ 125 mL	160 g

INDEX